NEW AND OLD

Writings by and about St. Nikolai Velimirovich

Ἀπαρχὴ Χριστός, μεσότης καὶ τελειότης· ἐν πᾶσι γὰρ ὁ ἐν τοῖς πρώτοις, ἔν τε τοῖς μέσοις καὶ τελευταίοις ὡς ἐν τοῖς πρώτοις ἐστίν· τὰ πάντα καὶ ἐν πᾶσι Χριστός

Christ is the beginning, the middle, and the end. He Who is in the first is in all, and as He is in the first so He is in the middle and the end as well—Christ is all and in all.

St. Symeon the New Theologian (*Chapters* 3.1).

TREASURES NEW AND OLD

Writings by and about St. Nikolai Velimirovich

Edited by
Bishop Maxim (Vasiljevic)

SEBASTIAN PRESS
2010

Published by
Sebastian Press
Western American Diocese of the Serbian Orthodox Church
in collaboration with The Institute for Theological Research in Belgrade

Edited by
Bishop Maxim (Vasiljevic)

Contemporary Christian Thought Series, number 8
First Edition

Prepress & printing
Interklima-grafika, Vrnjacka Banja

Address all correspondence to:
Sebastian Press
1621 West Garvey Avenue
Alhambra, California 91803

E-mail: info@westsrbdio.org ∴ Website: http://www.westsrbdio.org

Publishers Cataloging in Publication

Treasures new and old : writings by and about St. Nikolai Velimirovich / [edited by] Bishop Maxim Vasiljevic. — Alhambra, Calif. : Sebastian Press/Western American Diocese of the Serbian Orthodox Church, c2010.

p. 167 ; 23 cm.

ISBN: 978-0-9719505-9-7
Includes bibliographical references.

1. Velimirovic, Nikolaj, 1880–1956. 2. Orthodox Eastern Church—Serbia-Bishops—Biography. 3. Philosophy and religion. 4. Christian life—Orthodox Eastern authors. I. Velimirovic, Nikolaj, 1880–1956. Selections. English. II. Vasiljevic, Maxim. III. Title.

BX719.V45 T74 2010 — 2010940604
281.9092—dc22 — 1012

Contents

Part Three

A Century of Love

Part Four

Contemporary Testimonies

Foreword

by Bishop Maxim (Vasiljevic)

Before us is a book about a theologian, a minister, a missionary, a writer, a poet, an apostle, a saint, a man of dialogue: this book is about St. Nikolai Velimirovich, Bishop of Ohrid and Zhicha (1880–1956), who along with his many other attributes is regarded, with good reason, as an Enlightener of the Americas. The renewed interest in this man and his works has resulted in the materialization of this book for English-speaking readers who wish to become acquainted with this extraordinary person. The collected texts provide an extensive overview of his life, present important testimonies about his personality, and offer essential insights into his theology. The authors penetrate the depths of his thought with remarkable precision and also elucidate his actions. The authors agree that the appearance of Nikolai Velimirovich marks an era of change in the ecclesiastical and theological *paradigm* as a result of his spirituality, ecclesiastical work, and theological position. The amount of his written work alone is awe-inspiring (it comprises thirty volumes), and the task of specifying the content of the various themes is quite complex. The significance and relevance of his books are time-resistant; moreover, his works gain in importance each day.

The manner in which the person of Nikolai is perceived is another special feature of the present book. The authors in this collection of texts declare that it is high time to stop speaking about him in a journalistic manner with a pious-ethnic rhetorical tone. This, actually, results in obscuring and undermining the spiritual, theological, and philosophical magnitude of Nikolai as a thinker. Nikolai has bequeathed a singular theological legacy that exceeds the established perceptions of his time. The events that took place in Serbia after Nikolai's lifetime—that is, in the second half and particularly at the end of the twentieth century—led to the emergence of a contemporary and creative Orthodox self-consciousness following a complex and painful period of "Babylonian slavery" with all its repercussions. We say "slavery" because Florovsky's anatomical analysis of the impact of the long-standing subjugation of Orthodox ecclesiastical consciousness to Western "religionization" of the Church is very convincing. Its result is tragic: the renunciation of Orthodox consciousness is followed by a submission to rationalism, individualism, and to the ideologizing and secularization of the Faith. It is clear that the new political and economical conditions of twentieth-century mankind have exerted relentless pressures on Orthodox life, compelling its adaptation to the new circumstances. And so, the Orthodox Church has wandered into developmental currents that are unfamiliar and hitherto unknown in its history; the effects still need to be examined.

This book is of particular significance to the Western hemisphere of our planet Earth. As Metropolitan Amphilochius, one of the authors of this book, observes: "From the very beginning Bishop Nikolai was a European, well-inclined toward all Slavs and toward all men equally. He closely followed the theological, spiritual, scientific, and social events of his time." Hence, he showed a genuine concern for the whole universe, to which his entire life attests and which is exemplified by the following important words about America shortly before his death: "I came from the Old World to this New World. Which one of the two is better, the New one or the Old one? I cannot tell. However, the One Who revealed all truths told both you and me that a wise host brings both new and old things out of his treasury (cf. Matt. 13:52). Not just the new or merely the old, but both. Our Lord Jesus Christ honored the Old Testament and at the same time He revealed the New Testament to us. Now we, His followers, safeguard the one and the other as a singular Holy Book. The greatest wisdom consists in protecting the old and the new treasures alike. The separation of one from the other only leads to poverty, insecurity and confusion."

Nikolai's work in North America has not been sufficiently studied. From the autumn of 1921, he was the administrator of the newly established Serbian Diocese (with all the Church organs and in accordance with the Church canons) of the United States and Canada, and he remained in America until 1923. Following World War II he returned to America, and spent the final years of his life—his longest sojourn—in the United States, until his death. During the course of his many visits he participated in peace conferences, church ecumenical meetings and gatherings (the meeting of the World Council of Churches [WCC] in Evanston in 1952), at conferences of Christian youth of the world, and at Pan-Orthodox councils. He participated in Christian heterodox Church events, like, for example, the ordination and installation of his old friend (since 1915), Rev. William Manning as the tenth Episcopalian bishop of New York.

As an unfathomable humanist, Nikolai wrote the "*Orations on the Universal Man*" as an attempt to unite the ideas of pan-anthropism and pan-humanism. P. Bigovich observes: "The Universal Man was the counterpart to Nietzsche's notion of the "Übermensch," i.e., the Superman. While Nietzsche's Übermensch incorporated the deepest aspirations of Western European Cartesian metaphysical subjectivism, the Universal Man incorporated the deepest aspirations of the Balkans and Mediterranean man, of the Slavic man and of the man from the Far East... The goal was the establishment of the world upon Christian foundations, an introduction and a demonstration of Orthodoxy as the catholic Truth in its fullness—that is, in short, its deconfessionalization." The text "To Be and to Work," which was, in fact, a sermon delivered at the Anglican Church of Mercy in New York on May 6, 1946, discusses East-West relations with utmost discernment, reconciling ontology and ethics: "Look at our Lord and Savior. The East and the West met in Him in an extraordinary way. He was a perfect Easterner and at the same time a perfect Westerner. He was both a perfect Asian and a perfect American." He optimistically adds: "I hope that America will astonish the world by its spiritual awakening and by its Christian strength and greatness, just as it has astonished the world by its material development and scientific inventions." And this all-Orthodox American (and therefore Western) saint, this Easterner full of compassion for his Western brethren, ends his sermon with the following words of encouragement and Christian hope: "May our Merciful God grant you the mercy to go from glory to glory; may the Holy Spirit inspire you to be and to work according to the teachings of our Lord Jesus Christ."

Nikolai left his American counterparts with an impression of himself as an unbiased man, a man who was free of prejudice. According to the Canon N. West, prior to the arrival of Archimandrite Nikolai in 1915 the Anglican community had regarded the "exotic Orthodox faith" as something very remote. In his "Recollections of Bishop Nikolai", he writes that it was actually Bishop Nikolai who revealed Orthodoxy to the other branches of Christianity in both England and America.

An eloquent example of Nikolai's frankness and of his Pan-Orthodoxy is his willingness to view the Serbian Orthodox Church in America within the context of the ancient all-Orthodox Canonical Tradition, which is most eloquently exemplified by his prophetic words: "A time may not be far off when there will be a United Orthodox Church in America, which will include all the present Eastern national Churches in this country, a Church with one central administrative authority. I see in each of our now individual Churches a tendency toward such an end... And when by God's Providence the time will be ripe for the accomplishment of such a unity, I do not dare to doubt that the venerable heads of all our Orthodox Churches in Europe, Asia, and Africa, always led by the Holy Spirit, will give their blessing for the organization of a new autonomous sister Church in America" ("The Eastern Orthodox Church in America and Its Future," *Orthodoxy, Herald of the Serbian Orthodox Church in USA,* 1961, no. 3).

Nikolai's awareness of the need for "enculture-rezation"—that is, for preaching and witnessing the Gospel in ways which meet the cultural needs of the people—led him to the creation of highly exemplary and contemporary works, significant even in our postmodern era. His entire life struggle was a process of contextualizing the Evangelical message of the Resurrected Christ. His ardent desire was for the whole world to recognize the Orthodox salvific truth of the Resurrected God-Man Christ, Who is revealed and given in His Body, the Church.

Bishop Maxim of Western America
On the feast of St. Justin (Popovich) the New of Chelije, 2010

TROPARION

SAINT NIKOLAI OF ZHICHA AND OHRID

Tone 8.

Golden-mouthed preacher of the Resurrected Christ,
Guide of the cross-bearing Serbian people through the ages,
Resonant lyre of the Holy Spirit,
Pride and love of monastics, joy and glory of priests,
Teacher of repentance, bishop of the whole nation.
Leader of the God-praying army of Christ,
O holy Nikolai of Serbia and all Orthodoxy.
With all the saints in Heavenly Serbia,
Pray the Only Lover of mankind
To grant peace and unity to our people.

KONTAKION

SAINT NIKOLAI OF ZHICHA AND OHRID

Tone 3.

Born in Serbian Lelich,
You were the archpastor in St. Naum's Ohrid.
You presided from the throne of St. Sava in Zhicha,
By the Gospel you instructed and enlightened the people of God.
You led many to repentance and love for Christ.
For Christ's sake you endured suffering in Dachau;
For all this, O Saint, He glorified you,
Nikolai, the New God-pleasing One!

Saint Nikolai of Zhicha and Ohrid
(Icon by monks of Dechani, painted for the occasion of the translation of his relics to Zhicha, on the feast of St. Nicholas the Wonderworker, 2002)

PART ONE

Bishop Artemije (Radosavljevich)

The New Chrysostom Bishop Nikolai 1880–1956

Translated by Sister Michaela (Vavich)

Saint Nikolai of Zhicha
(Work of iconographer Petar Bilic, 2002)

The New Chrysostom

Thirty[1] years have passed since Bishop Nikolai departed from this world to a much better one, to God's eternal world. Long before, however, this great man from Lelich, the Bishop of Ohrid and Zhicha of blessed repose, was rightfully known as our *New Chrysostom*

On this thirtieth anniversary of his repose, it is my pleasure to reveal some more facts about him than are generally known to the people of Lelich in particular, to the Serbian people in general, and to the Orthodox and Christian world at large. I am aware of my modest means in contrast to the complexities and greatness of the person and works of Bishop Nikolai. However, as his closest compatriot and neighbor, I will attempt to present his evangelical life and his varied and prolific pastoral work, beginning with his birth in Lelich in 1880 and ending with his blessed repose in America in 1956.

His Life

Nikolai first glimpsed this world at the dawn of December 23 (Old Calendar) in 1880, the day before Christmas Eve, on the feast of St. Naum of Ohrid. He was born in the small yet "God-possessed village of Lelich," as he used to call it, not far from Valjevo, situated on the slopes of the Povlen Mountain. His parents, Dragomir and Katarina, were simple peasants, good and honest people, and pious Christians, especially his mother. Soon after his birth, they baptized their frail first-born son and gave him the name Nikola. A well-known priest of that time, Andrija, baptized him at the Chelije Monastery, which also served as Lelich's parish church.

Little Nikola grew strong in body and spirit in his parents' home, along with the rest of their nine children. (However, all the other children died or lost their lives in the war, so that only Nikola was left.) He received

[1] The first edition of "The New Chrysostom" was published in Belgrade, 1986.

his first impressions of God and the Orthodox Faith from his pious mother. He frequently accompanied her on the three-mile walk to the Chelije Monastery for prayers and Holy Communion. These first impressions about God, God's temple, and prayer, which Nikola fervently absorbed from his mother's lips, became firmly imprinted on his little soul.[2]

His father took little Nikola to the monastery of Chelije to learn to read and write so that he would at least "know how to read and reply to summons from the authorities," and remain in the village as the family provider and an "educated" man. However, Divine Providence had another, undeniably better plan in store for little Nikola, who from his earliest days demonstrated his extraordinary talent and zeal for learning. According to one account, Nikola used to retreat to a corner of the monastery's belfry and spend his school "recess" diligently reading and praying while the other children played and engaged in childish pranks.

His teacher Mihajlo Stuparevich noticed his exceptional zeal and ability and recommended that he continue his secondary education in Valjevo. Nikola proved to be the best student among his classmates. Like most students at that time, he too had to earn his expenses by providing domestic services in the town.

Following the completion of the tenth grade of his secondary education, Nikola applied for entrance to the Military Academy. However, he was rejected after failing the medical board examination due to his "small" stature, and because he did not meet the required chest circumference. This, too, was certainly due to Divine Providence, which was directing Nikola to another path, to become a soldier of the Heavenly King, and not of an earthly one. Immediately following his rejection by the medical board, Nikola submitted his transcripts to the Belgrade Theological Seminary and was admitted, but not without some difficulties, due to his alleged poor musical aptitude.

As a student of the seminary, he surpassed all his classmates during his studies. His outstanding performance in the sciences was the result of his God-given natural intelligence and his steadfast and systematic labor and effort. He well knew what a sin it is to bury God's talent in the earth and so he made a constant effort to multiply the talents he had received to the

[2] Later in his life Nikolai recollects those moments from his early childhood in his autobiographical writing "The Prayer of a Slave in Prison" (Prayerful Poems: Monk Thaddeus and Others [Munich, 1952], p. 70).

fullest. In his academic studies, he went beyond the prescribed textbooks and read many other works pertaining to general knowledge of secular and cultural significance. By the age of twenty-four, he had already read the works of Njegosh, Shakespeare, Goethe, Voltaire, Hugo, Nietzsche, Marx, Pushkin, Tolstoy, Dostoevsky, and many other great thinkers. He especially distinguished himself in the seminary by his novel thoughts on Njegosh, whom he admired as a poet and thinker and whom he had carefully studied during his secondary education in Valjevo. Young Nikola won the admiration of his colleagues and professors at the Belgrade Seminary, particularly for his ability to deliver speeches. One of many examples of his brilliant speeches is his farewell speech at the graduation luncheon of the seminary, held at the Rakovica Monastery in 1902.

During his studies in Belgrade, Nikola lived under harsh conditions, mainly due to poor food and the damp conditions of his living quarters. As a result, he was afflicted with scrofula, suffering from this for many years. Upon graduating the seminary, he took up short-term teaching positions in the villages of Drachich and Leskovice, not far from Valjevo. Here, he acquired first-hand knowledge of the life of our Serbian peasant and the disposition of his soul. He also became friends with the priest Sava Popovich, a refugee from Montenegro, helping him in the pastoral care of his parish. At the advice of his doctors, Nikola spent his summer holidays by the seaside, giving him the opportunity to become well acquainted with the life of the local people of Boka Kotorska, Montenegro, and Dalmatia, which he later lovingly described in his writings. During his seminary years he had already assisted the renowned priest, Aleksa Ilich, in editing the *Christian News* journal; his first letters and articles were published in this journal.

Along with the other graduated seminarians, Nikola was awarded a stipend from the government, and was selected by the Church authorities to continue his education in Russia or Europe. He chose to study in Europe, at the ancient Catholic faculty in Bern, and later on in Germany, England, and Switzerland. After his studies in those countries, he spent some time in Russia. He eagerly gathered knowledge from everywhere and acquired the broadest and best education of his time. Spiritually, he overcame many challenges and surpassed the mysterious wisdom of the Far East after plunging himself into the sacred and philosophical literature of ancient India. He had the ability to condense and process the knowledge he had gained deep into his soul and intellect from copious sources, and then present and impart it to the public in a most original and novel way, which became characteristic of him. Consequently, even the shortest text, his every spoken and written word, revealed an unusually rare erudition and intellect. Only the intellect of a true genius could harvest such a rich treasure of knowledge and wisdom and have the ability to express it in a most unique way.

At the age of twenty-eight, Nikola crowned his studies in Bern with a doctorate in theology, after defending his dissertation "Faith in the Resurrection of Christ as the Fundamental Dogma of the Apostolic Church."[3] In fact, the events that followed and the rest of his life would prove his faithfulness to the sign of the Cross and of Christ's Resurrection. In 1909, Nikola was at Oxford University, where he prepared his doctorate in philosophy. However, it was in Geneva that he defended his dissertation, "The Philosophy of Berkeley," in French.

Upon his return from Europe, Nikola became very ill after contracting dysentery and was hospitalized for six weeks. He then said to himself, "If my service to God is needed, He will save me." And so he vowed that if he recovered he would enter monasticism and in this way serve God and His people in the Church. He was already a distinguished Doctor of theology and philosophy when he was tonsured a monk with the name of Nikolai, and ordained a hieromonk in Rakovica Monastery on December 20, 1909. Thus, he wholeheartedly placed himself, his knowledge and his abilities at the service of God and the Serbian nation.

After he returned from his studies, he submitted his foreign diplomas for validation in accordance with the laws of his time. However, his secondary education was found incomplete, and so he was compelled to take the exams of the final two years of high school and also pass the university entrance exam in order to be accepted as a teacher at the Theological Seminary. According to one member of the examination commission, "Listening to his discourse on Christ left everyone speechless and nobody asked him another question." Nevertheless, before accepting a teaching position at the Theological Seminary, he was sent to Russia by Metropolitan Dimitrije, where he spent the following year traveling

[3] This work was published in Bern, Germany in 1910; the translated Serbian version was published in the Bishop's *Collected Works*, vol. 2 (Himmelstür, 1986).

around the vast Russian lands, becoming acquainted with her church life, with the Russian soul, and with Russia's sanctuaries and holy places. During this period, Nikolai wrote his first major work, namely, his study "The Religion of Njegosh."

As a teacher at St. Sava's Seminary in Belgrade, Nikolai taught philosophy, logic, psychology, history, and foreign languages. However, he could not be confined to the life of the seminary; the walls of the classrooms were too restrictive for him. This is how his writings, speeches, and publications emerged. The young and learned Hieromonk soon began his brilliant orations in Belgrade's churches and other churches all around Serbia. These sermons were followed by lectures, which he delivered at the Kolarchevo University. He spoke primarily about topics from everyday life but in an unprecedented manner, unheard of until then; his speeches took Serbia's intellectual community by storm. During this period, Nikolai published his articles, sermons, and studies in church and other literary journals; his subject matter included Njegosh, Nietzsche, and Dostoevsky, as well as other philosophical and theological topics.[4]

His strong church, religious, and national-public remarks in the liberal-democratic Serbia of that time caused waves of admiration and respect from many people. However, he already had a growing number of enemies and of people who envied him. The young hieromonk and learned orator Nikolai had become popular and was the talk of many, not only in Belgrade and Serbia, but also in all the other Yugoslav regions.[5] And so in 1912 he was invited to the celebration of the anniversary of the journal "Prosveta," where he aroused the enthusiasm of the youth of Bosnia and Hercegovina and where he became acquainted with the most prominent representatives of the enslaved Serbs of that time: Chorovich, Duchich, Shantich, Grgich, Ljubibratich, and others. His famous words, "Through their great love and big hearts, the Serbs of Bosnia have

[4] Nikolai's study "The Religion of Njegosh" was first published in the journal "Delo," and as a separate publication in 1911. It has been evaluated as the most brilliant study of the great Njegosh. Further publications of this work appeared in 1921 and in 1971. Nikolai's keen interest in Njegosh continued, and in 1922, on the occasion of the translation of Njegosh's remains to the restored chapel of St. Peter of Cetinje at Lovchen, his speech was especially remarkable and singled out. Unfortunately, today this chapel no longer exists because it was dismantled. [This occurred under the Communist regime, which erected a memorial on the site of his grave.—TRANS.]

[5] Yugo means south; slav pertains to the Slavic peoples.—TRANS.

annexed Serbia to Bosnia," resounded very provocatively to the Austrian authorities[6] who, in fact, had Nikolai removed from the train on his return to Belgrade for several days of questioning. The same Austrian authorities prevented him from attending the celebration of Njegosh's anniversary in Zagreb the following year. Nevertheless, his speech reached Zagreb and was read. According to Dedijer (in his work "The Assassination Attempt in Sarajevo"), the young Bosnians were so taken by Nikolai that they used to take their oaths on Nikolai's work "The Sermons at the Foot of the Mount" instead of the Gospel.

Nikolai continued his national work with an even greater zeal as tiny Serbia began her ascent to Golgotha in the ensuing wars for the liberation and unification of the Serbian and other Yugoslav peoples. He actively and personally participated in those fateful days of the wars from 1912 to 1918. With watchful eyes and a vigilant soul, he followed the development of events both at the front and in the rear lines of the battlefields. He conducted talks, delivered speeches to encourage and console the people in their superhuman struggles and afflictions, and contributed his services as a volunteer in providing aid to the war victims, the sick and the poor in those difficult times of war. He also renounced his salary in favor of the government for the duration of the war. His speeches during this period, compiled in *Above Sin and Death,* are comparable to those of Pericles of the ancient Helladic age, spoken to glorify those fallen for their country.

Nikolai was equally active in the life of the Church. His constructive criticisms, aimed at the work and behavior of certain church people were, in essence, critical observations reflecting his positive attitude toward the Church, an attitude that remained constant throughout his life. As one consequence, Nikolai parted with Rev. Father Aleksa, ending their joint collaboration on the *Christian News* journal because of the latter's unhelpful views on the situation of the Serbian Church. Nikolai's prophetic spirit as an apostle and shepherd of his people far exceeded that of all his opponents and the envious, with whom he had to contend all his life and even after his death. Nikolai, however, always forgave readily and easily.[7]

[6] Bosnia and Hercegovina were annexed to the Austro-Hungarian monarchy during its occupation, which lasted until World War I.—TRANS.

[7] See Appendix I, *Prayers by the Lake*, LXXV, in which Nikolai blesses his enemies as his benefactors.—TRANS.

In April of 1915, the Serbian government sent Nikolai on a national mission from Nish to America and England in service of the Serbian and southern Slavic national interests. He remained abroad on this mission until April 1919, promoting the Serbian cause through his characteristic wisdom and eloquence, and taking advantage of his knowledge of foreign languages and his popularity. He was able to impart the truth about the Serbian Golgotha to the Western Allies; he talked both about the weaknesses of the Serbian people, which the Austro-Hungarian propaganda had over-exaggerated, and also about the virtues of the Serbian soul, which the same enemies had repressed.

He gave numerous lectures in America and later in England,[8] at churches, universities, hotels and other venues in his campaign for the salvation and unification of the Serbs and Southern Slavic peoples. Already by August 1915, at a big rally in Chicago, he had united and won over a great number of people and clerics to the Yugoslav cause (the program of the Yugoslav Committee), including Roman Catholics, Uniates, and Protestants who, separately from the Orthodox, publicly expressed their desire for the liberation and unification of Serbia. Subsequently, a significant number of volunteers from America headed for the front at Thessalonica. The view (of the Commander-in-Chief of the British Army) that "Fr. Nikolai comprised the third army" of the Serbian and Southern Slavic cause was not without foundation because his contribution was, in fact, considerable. It was also during this period that Nikolai presented the idea of the unification of all Christian churches, befriending especially the Anglican and Episcopalian Churches. At the same time, Nikolai, who had previously lectured in England, also provided assistance to a group of Serbian students at Oxford.

While still in England at the end of the war, Nikolai was elected Bishop of Zhicha on March 12/25.[9] Subsequently he was transferred to the Bishopric of Ohrid toward the end of 1920. During this period he was sent on many ecclesiastical and political missions, taking him to Athens, Constantinople, Holy Mount Athos, England, and America. Well documented

[8] Nikolai Velimirovich, *Serbia in Light and Darkness,* with a Preface by the Archbishop of Canterbury (London: Longmans, Green and Co., 1916; repr., New York: Cosimo Classics, 2007): a compilation of Nikolai's lectures first published in English in 1916. See Appendix II.—TRANS.

[9] There are thirteen days difference between the New and the Old Calendars, that is, between the Gregorian and Julian Calendars.—TRANS.

and witnessed by many people, Nikolai's missionary endeavors were very productive. Nikolai participated in peace conferences, church-ecumenical meetings and assemblies, conferences of Christian world youth organizations, and pan-Orthodox conferences.

A special emphasis, however, should be placed on Nikolai's pastoral and spiritual labors in Ohrid and Bitolj, and later on in 1934 when he was reappointed to Zhicha, according to the wishes of the Holy Synod of Bishops and the people. Around this time, while serving as Bishop of Ohrid and Zhicha, Nikolai's work in all areas of Church and public life reached its full potential without his theological and literary work suffering neglect. Furthermore, he contributed significantly to the unification of the local Serbian churches in the territory of the newly established state that often neither supported nor understood his efforts.

Ancient Ohrid, the cradle of Slavonic literacy and culture in the Balkans, had a special influence on Bishop Nikolai; he described it as "the sacred city with its great and fertile past and its very constrained present." Orthodox Russia, with her sacred places and holy ascetics, had already made a great impact on Nikolai. This positive influence was now reinforced and completed by the pious Ohrid, and by the neighboring Mount Athos, which Deda-Vladyka[10] visited each summer. The Holy Mountain of Athos and the works of the Holy Fathers, avidly read and profoundly studied by Nikolai during this period, imparted to him for life his deep roots in Orthodoxy. Here, during this period of his life, he underwent a profound and fundamental inner change, emanating from him in a tangible way and openly observed by simple and pious folk. This spiritual turning point manifested itself in everything: in Nikolai's speech, behavior, even in his attire. In his earlier days, the young Hieromonk, Dr. Nikolai Velimirovich, had striven to impress, charm and attract everyone. In his "pre-Ohrid" period, Nikolai could typically be depicted as dressed in shining priest's cassocks, with well-groomed hair and elegant manners, eloquent and very sophisticated in his discourses. As such, we experience him in his work *Words on the Complete Man*, a rare and profoundly brilliant book of recent Serbian literature. Brilliant from a philosophical point of view, it is, however, not as spiritual or completely and profound-

[10] *Deda* and *Vladyka* are endearing term for grandfather and bishop respectively.—Trans.

ly Orthodox as his works that followed his time in Ohrid and Zhicha (*Homilies, The Prologue of Ohrid, Missionary Letters*), along with his pastoral and spiritual work with the Orthodox people, the Bogomoljci,[11] and the monastic communities.

During this second period of his life, Nikolai cast away from himself and from his people all forms of the alienation and superficialities of Western societies. He was completely imbued with the warm current of Orthodoxy; captivated and enraptured by the crucified and salvific image of Christ and by what St. Sava[12] had wrought for the Church and her people. Worldly glory was meaningless to him; the praise of men, distasteful; elaborate literary expression, akin to idle talk; and he regarded worldly wisdom as spiritual poverty and deficiency. This does not mean, however, that the Bishop became a simpleton. He became simple through his spirituality. To him, Christ's words: *I am the Way, the Truth and the Life* (John 14:6) became all and everything. He turned away from the world toward his inner self and toward his people who were thirsting for God. A genuine inner rebirth had taken place, a new birth; the beginning of a holy life had emerged. Christ is the One Who gave him and the souls around him a new birth. So, Nikolai the man of genius became Nikolai the Saint. It was exactly this transformation that attracted people to him, causing them to gather around him. Unfortunately, Nikolai was not without enemies, slanderers, and schemers, even during this period of his life. Nevertheless, both earlier and later, he overcame everything with his transparent and simple life, accompanied by his works before God and his people.

Had this transition in Ohrid and Zhicha not taken place, Nikolai would have most likely remained merely a great and lonely genius among the Serbian people: like a lone pine tree somewhere in the mountains

[11] A movement of pious Serbian Orthodox lay people who gathered together in prayer, Bible studies, evangelism, and charitable work under the patronage of Bishop Nikolai. Many of the children of these pious people became monastics and had a major impact on the revival of monasticism in Serbia following the five hundred years of the Turkish/Muslim and Austro-Hungarian/Catholic occupations.—TRANS.

[12] St. Sava, the son of the first ruler and founder of the medieval Serbian state, Stefan Nemanja, united all the Serbian principalities ecclesiastically in the early thirteenth century. He established the autocephalous Serbian Orthodox Church with the blessing of the Ecumenical Patriarch of Constantinople and was consecrated as the first Archbishop in 1219. This sealed the supremacy of Orthodox Christianity in the Serbian realm.—TRANS.

without an equal or a rival. He would never have become the people's Deda-Vladyka or the holy Deka,[13] the New Serbian Chrysostom—a Chrysostom not only in word and speech but also in deed, in his pastoral and apostolic work, and as a confessor of Christ. Like St. Sava long ago, Nikolai had gradually become the light and holy conscience of the entire Serbian nation, of his own generation and of the generations to come. For the Serbian people had accepted and had undeniably adopted Bishop Nikolai as their spiritual guide, as God's prophet and saint. No one will ever be able to drive him out of the heart and soul of the faithful or erase his memory. With regard to his past and recent critics, the Bishop himself demonstrated how one should act in the following incident. A journalist from *Politika* interviewed Nikolai in Zhicha and invited him to comment on a serious affront and insult hurled at him by another bishop. The journalist wrote, "Bishop Nikolai stared at me for a long time without saying anything. That look and his silence were clearer than any answer could ever have been" (*Politika,* no. 11344 [Nov. 29, 1939]).

The main body of Nikolai's work, which we will refer to later, originates from this period. Here we should at least mention his other achievements of no lesser significance, such as his pastoral and charitable works, and other activities for the general good of the people; his work with pious people, the Bogomoljci[14] in particular, his efforts at the renewal of destroyed, deserted or half-empty monasteries in the Dioceses of Ohrid, Bitolj, and Zhicha; his renewal and erection of cemeteries, memorials, public

[13] Like Deda, Deka is another endearing term for grandfather.—Trans.

[14] We shall present here a passage which Nikolai wrote about the Bogomoljci (excerpt from his sermon at the Synod in 1940, "The Hearth of Faith in Today's Darkness"): "At that time a group of people appeared among the Serbian people who others called the Bogomoljci. These people cared about nothing other than God and their souls; their main principle was: Begin with yourself! They read the Holy Scriptures, sang spiritual songs, met in prayer, went on pilgrimages to monasteries, confessed their sin in true repentance, fasted and took Holy Communion, talked about the miracles God had done in their lives. This is how they overcame the passions within themselves. They were despised, mocked, persecuted, arrested, tortured (in pre-war Yugoslavia—A.R.) but they paid no attention to all of that. They were called lunatics. I was also called a lunatic. Those who called me that said: is it possible that Nikolai who has spent such a long time in enlightened England associates himself now with those lunatics? They did not know that England has only strengthened my faith and my prayer life. So when they called me a lunatic, I rejoiced. May God never allow this "lunacy" to grow weaker in me until the end of my life" (*Collected Works*, vol. 11 [Himmelstur, 1983], p. 556).

drinking fountains, and other charitable and public institutions and memorials. A special emphasis should be placed on his work with poverty-stricken children and students, and his establishment of orphanages and shelters for deprived children, independent of their ethnicity and religion, which has remained public knowledge to this day. Deka's well-known "Bogdaj"[15] in Bitolj was successfully run by Nada Adjich, later known as Mother Ana, the Abbess of the monastery of Vrachevshnjici. (One of Bishop Nikolai's children's poems stems from Bogdaj: We are little Bitoljchani/the tiny underprivileged ones/our house lies at the very far end/in Bogdaj like in Heaven,/ in Bogdaj.) Nikolai opened similar children's shelters in the cities of Kraljevo, Chachak, Gornji Milanovac and Kragujevac, in which over six hundred deprived children were placed before the war.

While in Ohrid and Zhicha, Nikolai also developed a multi-faceted Pan-Orthodox and inter-church program. In 1930, he participated in the Pre-Synodal Conference of the Orthodox Churches in the monastery of Vatopedi. He also worked on the renewal of the coenobitic way of life in Hilandar Monastery. He often participated in international meetings of the World Christian Youth as well as in a number of ecumenical meetings and world conferences. He nurtured a good relationship with the Orthodox brethren of Bulgaria and Greece, who were equally important to him. He strove for good inter-Christian and inter-faith relationships in pre-War Yugoslavia.[16] Unfortunately, however, due to the anti-Orthodox and anti-Serb politics of the Stojadinovich regime, Nikolai had to become involved in the infamous "Concordat,"[17] imposed upon the Serbian faithful and upon the Church by the regime and police of Stojadinovich and Koroshec.[18] The victory in this struggle and the ensuing dismantling

[15] The name of the orphanage means: (May the) Lord grant.—TRANS.

[16] The Serbs and their lands were completely freed from the five-hundred-year Turkish occupation only following World War I, in which one-third of the nation perished. However, because the Western Allies would not permit the formation of the Kingdom of Serbia in the ensuing peace treaties, the Kingdom of the Serbs, Croats and Slovenes was formed instead, which later, during the reign of King Alexander Karadjordjevich, became the Kingdom of Yugoslavia, and lasted until World War II.—TRANS.

[17] Bishop Nikolai successfully campaigned against the Yugoslav government's intentions of signing a concordat with the Vatican, which would have given special privileges to the Roman Catholic Church.—TRANS.

[18] Among other things is the well-known telegram and open letter of Nikolai addressed to "Mr. Dr. Anton Koroshec, Minister of the Interior," dated August 1937. In

of the Concordat was to a great extent the work of Bishop Nikolai; it had broad reverberations among the masses of the Serbian faithful. Nikolai, beside Patriarch Gavrilo, also played a role in the collapse of the anti-national pact of the Cvetkovich-Machek government.[19] For this the Serbian people paid him special tribute, while the occupying Germans[20] especially hated him.

With great love, the Serbian people closely followed Nikolai's work, his every word, written or verbal. His works are still read, reproduced, retold and will long be remembered. Even today, you can hear many of Nikolai's sayings, his edifying words and anecdotes retold by the people. Father Rafael from Ovchar used to say, "Every word of his was worthy of the Psalter." Nikolai's wealth in God won over the Serbian soul, enabling him to influence our people on such a grand scale. His evangelical influence aided the organism of the Serbian Church in enduring the suffering that lay ahead for her. Nikolai's importance was especially felt following World War II and is still felt to this very day; it will only continue to increase as time goes on.

Bishop Nikolai's prolific and extensive work for and influence on the health of the Serbian people and Church was interrupted by the inferno of World War II that engulfed our homeland, as witnessed by many of us, including those of us who were but children at the time. Old Yugoslavia's capitulation occurred while Bishop Nikolai was residing in Zhicha Monastery. The Bishop shared the same ominous fate with his holy Zhicha and with his people, who were torn apart and annihilated mercilessly, beginning with day one of the occupation.

In 1941, on the feast of Sts. Peter and Paul, the Germans arrested Nikolai. He was initially confined within the walls of the monastery of

it he lodges his complaint about "the wolf-like police attack on the peaceful Orthodox litany in front of the Cathedral Church in Belgrade of July 19," and about the persecution and arrests of many innocent Orthodox priests and faithful all over Yugoslavia.

[19] On August 26, 1939, a political agreement was settled between the Yugoslav prime minister, Dragisha Cvetkovich, and a Croat politician, Vladko Machek, to effectively create a Croatian sub state in Yugoslavia.—TRANS.

[20] On the occasion of March 27 [The anti-Nazi coup d'etat in Yugoslavia took place on March 27, 1941.—TRANS.] the citizens of the city of Kraljevo addressed a telegram congratulating Bishop Nikolai in Belgrade ,which he answered with another telegram with the following words: "Grateful to God, thankful to the people, we now look forward to a bright future without the stain of shame" (*Pastirski glas,* no. 3, 1941).

Ljubostinja and later transferred to the monastery of Vojlovica near the town of Panchevo, where he was placed under strict house-arrest along with the Serbian Patriarch, Gavrilo Dozich, and guarded by heavily armed German soldiers. Bishop Nikolai did not suffer as much physically; his soul suffered much more during his imprisonment. He spent days and nights in prayer, crying out to God for help for his people and all of humanity. (Nikolai's supplicatory canon and prayer to the Most Holy Theotokos of Vojlovac have been preserved, as well as some of his later writings like the renowned "Three Prayers in the Shadow of German Bayonets," written in January 1945 on the inside covers of the Gospels, now preserved at the Serbian Church in Vienna.)

On September 14, 1944, the Germans transferred Bishop Nikolai and Patriarch Gavrilo from Vojlovica to their internment in the infamous concentration camp of Dachau, where they were detained until the end of the war. In Dachau, they experienced all the horrors of hell on earth. Many witnesses have testified to the suffering and agonies they endured there and the resulting permanent damage to their health; the hierarchs, too, testified in their own written and oral disclosures later. On May 8, 1945, both hierarchs were finally set free by the Thirty-sixth American Army Division of the Allied Forces. For a time they drifted from one Western country to another until Patriarch Gavrilo was finally able to return home and once again take his place at the helm of the Serbian Church. Nikolai, however, began his difficult and thorny course of emigration, forsaken and homeless in this wide world. He carried the warmth of his love for his people and his country in his heart and soul, which were torn apart by his profound nostalgia and his desire to be buried in his country.

In 1946, Nikolai arrived in America, nearly crushed by pain of soul and body. He was frequently ill, complaining of pain in his legs and back—the direct result of the suffering and torments of the concentration camp (according to the testimony of one Russian hieromonk, the personal attendant of the ailing Bishop).

Nevertheless, Nikolai found the strength to carry on his missionary and ecclesiastical work even in America, travelling the great distances of America and Canada, encouraging the faint-hearted, making peace among those who quarreled, and teaching the evangelical life and faith to those thirsting for God. The Orthodox and other Christians in America alike consider his missionary work as extremely important and have rightly included him in the ranks of the Apostles and Missionaries of the New World. Nikolai continued his missionary efforts and his theological work in both Serbian and English. His works such as *Cassiana, The Land of No Return, The Lord's Harvests, Conversations,* and his last unfinished work, *The Only Lover of Mankind,* stem from this period. Moreover, from America he sent aid to our monasteries and to needy individuals in the old country, as much as his means allowed, in the form of modest packages and monetary contributions. He also continued to provide help especially in Church matters.

In America, Bishop Nikolai taught temporarily at the provisional Serbian Theological Seminary at St. Sava Monastery in Libertyville, Illinois, at St. Vladimir's Seminary in New York, at the Holy Trinity Russian Theological Seminary at Jordanville, New York, and at St. Tikhon's Seminary at South Canaan, Pennsylvania, where he reposed at the beginning of Great Lent, early on Sunday, March 5/18, 1956. He had risen from bed to prepare himself through prayer for the celebration of the Divine Liturgy when he was taken from this world to the Heavenly Church to celebrate the eternal Heavenly Liturgy before God. On March 27, he was taken from St. Tikhon's Monastery to St. Sava's Monastery at Libertyville, and in the presence of a large number of Serbs and other faithful from all across the United States, he was laid to rest next to the church altar on the south side. Once the news of Deka's death reached our country, the bells of many churches and monasteries began to ring and the forty-day funeral and memorial services were held everywhere. Finally, I must make mention of Bishop Nikolai's publicly expressed desire to be brought to his beloved home for burial, "there where I first learned the alphabet," i.e., at the monastery of Chelije, in his beloved Lelich.

Literary and Theological Works

Exactly thirty years ago Bishop Nikolai passed from the earthly to the heavenly Serbia. However, he left his legacy to the Serbian people and to Serbia here on earth, that is, his literary, commemorative and spiritual works. This legacy bears the indelible seal of his Christ- and man-loving soul, and will forever be cherished by the Serbian people. His literary and theological works, in particular, occupy a special place.

Without question, Bishop Nikolai's works are more numerous and brilliant than any other Serbian author's. The Serbian Church and people will draw spiritually from these works for centuries to come. Internationally, Nikolai's writings, their volume, standard and quality, are on par with Origen, St. John Chrysostom and Blessed Augustine. Bishop Nikolai remains virtually without an equal even in the international community at large, which is demonstrated also by the diversity of his topics and the ease with which he developed them.

Here, we shall cite in chronological order only the major titles of Bishop Nikolai's works in order to give an idea of the extent of his literary corpus: *On the Resurrection of Christ* (1910), *On Boka Kotorska* (1910), *The Religion of Njegosh* (1911),*Sermons at the Foot of the Mount* (1912), *Beyond Sin and Death* (1914), *Orations on the Universal Man* (1920), *Prayers by the Lake* (1922), *New Sermons at the Foot of the Mount* (1922), *Thoughts on Good and Evil* (1923), *Homilies* (two volumes, 1925), *The Prologue of Ohrid* (1928), *War and the Bible* (1931), *The Faith of Educated People* (1931), *Symbols and Signs* (1932), *The King's Oath* (1933), *The Spiritual Lyre* (1934), *Emmanuel* (1937), *Homiletics* (1940), *The Land of No Return* (1950), *The Lord's Harvests* (1952), *Cassiana: The Science of Love* (1952), *Prayerful Poems: Monk Thaddeus and others* (1952), *Splendour: The Science of Miracles* (1953), *The Only Lover of Mankind* (1958), *The Lord's First Commandment and the Heavenly Pyramid* (1959). Many of his minor works include a large number of homilies, speeches, and articles. A certain number of the minor works of the Bishop have been published only in English and are, as yet, not translated in Serbian. Many Serbian journals and newspapers published before World War II contain articles, homilies, poems, and other texts by Bishop Nikolai.

If everything Bishop Nikolai wrote were to be published, it would comprise more than twenty large volumes.[21] The majority of his writings represent a precious wealth deposited into the spiritual treasury of the Serbian Church, people, and of all humanity. The study of the Bishop's literary, theological, and spiritual works as well as a study of him as a thinker is, of course, still in front of us. However, at present it is not possible to elaborate on each work separately here. We believe that the time will come when studies and doctoral theses will be written on Nikolai's works. We shall, however, at least provide an outline with some of the general characteristics of Nikolai's works.

First of all, the depth and strength of Bishop Nikolai's thought reflected in his works are profoundly philosophical, particularly those from his earlier writings, such as *The Religion of Njegosh* and *Orations on the Universal Man.* These works alone place Nikolai among the world-renowned philosophers. The only philosopher in our country who could be compared to Nikolai is Bishop Njegosh himself. Both men complement each other and harmonize with one another. After all, this is implied and understood in Nikolai's study of *The Religion of Njegosh.*

The content and the message of Nikolai's works are predominantly theological and spiritual. They are the outcome of the bishop's personality, which is permeated by true theology. Central to his thoughts and writings about God is Christ—the only Lover of mankind. Nikolai began his spiritually creative work with Him (his dissertation: "Faith in the Resurrection of Christ...") and finished his work with Him *(The Only Lover of Mankind).* Christ is the Beginning and the End, just like in the Apocalypse. However, with Nikolai, Christ is also everything in between. There is no doubt that Bishop Nikolai has joined the ranks of the Holy Church Fathers in his search for and glorification of God.

All of Nikolai's works are stylistically expressed in poetic-prose. His earlier works (*The Religion of Njegosh, Orations on the Universal Man,* and especially *Prayers by the Lake*) are vibrant in their lyrical mood, characterized by a Christian view of the cosmos. In his later works, his poetic creativity undergoes a change and is transformed into humble modesty, and draws

[21] Our Bishop Lavrentije of Western Europe has recently begun to publish the *Collected Works* of Bishop Nikolai, which so far comprise ten volumes. [The publication in Serbian has been completed since this biography was written.—TRANS.]

nearer to the Church poetry of the Holy Fathers. Examples of this are found in *The Spiritual Lyrics*, *Prayerful Poems*, and in his verses in *The Prologue of Ohrid*. Each verse in the *Prologue* contains a dogma, which virtually transforms the poem into a complete little dogmatic. His poems of *The Spiritual Lyrics* are presently chanted in Serbian Church services. In many churches and monasteries they are most frequently sung before Holy Communion during the Divine Liturgy. Their content and the folk melodies touch the simple heart and move it to tears. How many times has Fr. Justin,[22] touched by Nikolai's poems and songs, said in tears, "May St. Damascene forgive me, but Nikolai has surpassed him." Nikolai's poems have been especially dear to our pious Bogomoljci. They have become a regular collection of songs, sung at their gatherings and meeting places. Many people have experienced miraculous transformations through repentance motivated through these songs, and have changed their way of life, and found the path to salvation; some have chosen the monastic life by so doing. These songs and poems of Bishop Nikolai are a monumental legacy to future generations of pious Serbian people.

As a final point, all of Bishop Nikolai's literary work is immersed in an oratory spirit. His poems are sermons in verse, just as his works in prose are—poetry in their own way. Nikolai is an orator who has no equal or rival in the history of the Serbian people. Fr. Justin frequently and correctly pointed out that the "Serbian soul was just stuttering before Nikolai was born. He gave it expression, so that it could begin to speak." He is the only one in our generation who stands shoulder to shoulder with St. John Chrysostom; this is why Fr. Justin and others called him the "Serbian Chrysostom."

Until the appearance of Bishop Nikolai, oration in our country was crushed and had altogether died out. Sermons were delivered and spoken out of need, and were stereotypes. The oratorical gift of Nikolai of Ohrid and Zhicha was, therefore, experienced as a blessed rainfall in times of drought, like the heavenly manna in the desert, a true miracle and revelation. The topics of his sermons are varied, always contemporary and relevant, like those in the times of the holy Church Fathers that are read and experienced today as eternal and of permanent value.

[22] St. Justin Popovich (1894–1979). Blessed Elder of the Serbian Orthodox Church, theologian and philosopher; he studied under Bishop Nikolai as a student.—Trans.

Nikolai's orations moved and filled many with enthusiasm, creating a greater zeal in the preaching of the word of God. Through his unceasing and brilliant labors, Nikolai created a large group of orators among the people, "folk preachers." One Bogomoljac commented, "The world has never seen people in peasant jackets and shoes preaching the Gospels!" Some of the old "missionary preachers" still alive today continue to preach at well-attended gatherings of the Bogomoljci. Nikolai's entire life can be described as a powerful sermon about Christ our Lord and His Gospel.

A Contemporary Father of the Church

We have reviewed in short Bishop Nikolai's literary and theological legacy and have just started to become acquainted with him; for the works of a man are not the same as the man himself, just as the mouldboard is not the same as the blacksmith. Every work, a literary work in particular, is the fruit of a person; the man is the living person who creates the works. Therefore, as the true words of God's Logos affirm: *Every tree is known by his own fruit* (Luke 6:44); the person, also, is known by his works.

Everything Bishop Nikolai wrote, accomplished, and left behind is stored in the common treasury of God's Church, in the "pillar and fortress of the Truth," also containing the living works of the earlier Church Fathers of the past twenty centuries. There is no doubt that the Bishop dwells with them—in the Kingdom of Christ our Lord, with Whom and for Whom they all lived and worked here on earth.

If the expression of a contemporary Greek theologian is accurate, namely, that "the Church Fathers are the quintessence of great and colossal grace, continuing the works of the Holy Apostles, devoted to Christ in soul and body, well-tested and tried on the path of virtues, worthy of great illumination, and rightly administering the words of Truth through their own lives, through their preaching, and through their writings which overflowed with Divine wisdom," then Bishop Nikolai is undoubtedly among them. For everything that is said about them also applies to him. Patristic literature and the lives of the Holy Fathers are two of the most precious gems of the Church, after the Holy Scriptures. All of the writings of the Holy Church Fathers embody the great outpouring of their depth and insight into the word of God, not merely intellectually, but as evidenced by their lives. They fulfilled God's commandments in their lives, from the greatest to the least, and this is why their intellect was so illumined, and was able to rise to the mysteries of God's Revelations. The stature of their theology and their correct and precise dogmatic pronouncements is not merely explained by their constant study of the Holy Scriptures, but also because they lived by the Scriptures, which was their very breath.

For this reason the Holy Fathers have always been highly respected and esteemed in the Orthodox Church. This is also why Fr. Justin expressed the following in his writings: "We do not cease to emphasize that the Holy Fathers are the best thinkers of the Church because they think through the Holy Spirit." In like manner, Fr. Justin frequently spoke about Bishop Nikolai, his relationship with the Serbian people in particular, and crowned him with a glorious wreath, as only he was able to do. Fr. Justin used to call him the "the holy Bishop, the thirteenth Apostle, the fifth Evangelist, and undeniably the greatest Serb after St. Sava," because, "everything he bequeathed, everything that represents the best in us, the most sublime, the purest, the holiest, are all the fruits of his works..."; "In any case, we are thankful to the holy Serbian Apostle, Bishop Nikolai. Truly holy, Bishop Nikolai," Fr. Justin stated at Lelich on the twentieth anniversary of Bishop Nikolai's repose.

If we continue our research into the life and works of Bishop Nikolai, it is easy to detect some basic characteristics similar to those of the earlier Church Fathers and which place him among them.

First, he is a singular man of prayer and an intercessor for his people before God, like Moses the God-Seer. His entire life is nothing less than an uninterrupted act of prayer before God and in God. In a fashion similar to the Old Testament Psalmist, Bishop Nikolai poured out his prayerful soul in his works, especially in his *Prayers by the Lake*, in *The Spiritual Lyre*, and in *Prayerful Songs*. In his poetic fervor and inspiration, his poems compare to the Psalms like heavenly flowers. His prayerful spirit was so powerful that it often brought him to his knees with streams of tears flowing from his eyes, witnessed by those who frequently saw him and noticed that he often wept. His unquenchable thirst for God could be satisfied only with complete union with Him. The ascetic of Ohrid, inflamed by divine eros, expressed his longing for God especially powerfully in *Prayers by the Lake*. All of Nikolai's works are imbued with his prayerful sighs, his cries, and his longing for God; prayer was his very breath. His lips uttered prayers everywhere: in church, at home, on the road, in prison, and in the shadow of German bayonets.[23]

Prayer in Orthodox Christianity is the basic and primary means of purifying the heart and illumining the intellect. Hence, it is not surprising that the Orthodox Church's great men and women of prayer were all great visionaries endowed with the gift of prophesy. Bishop Nikolai was one of them. He foresaw and foretold events that after him many witnessed and experienced. He foretold how almighty Europe, the Europe he had known during his studies, would turn to dust if its Christian foundations were destroyed. However, something even worse happened. Europe not only turned into dust but into a slaughterhouse unknown in history, fuming and drowning in a sea of bloodshed of more than fifty million human beings, and shaking from the convulsions and screams of the slain and persecuted nations.

Bishop Nikolai's apocalyptic visions of Europe were introduced to the wider public by another great contemporary saint of ours, namely, by Fr. Justin, an ascetic and theologian. He presented them with his short commentaries in his book *The Orthodox Church and Ecumenism*, published in Thessalonica in 1974. Bishop Nikolai's in-depth visions express his perception of the last three centuries of European history (eighteenth, nineteenth, and twentieth) as a singular record of the trial of Christ by Europe; Europe ultimately casts Christ from itself and out of itself. Following this "judgment," the Bishop and Equal to the Apostles is quoted in his sorrowful announcement: "My brethren, the disputes have come to an end in our times. Christ has departed from Europe as He once did from Gadara at the request of the Gadarenes. But as soon as He left, war, fury, madness, destruction, and desolation appeared. The brutal Hunnish, Lombard, and African barbarism of pre-Christian Europe has returned once again, but with a hundredfold horror. Christ has taken His Cross and His blessing and has retreated. Only darkness and stench are left ... Europe has turned into the White Devil and the Europeans into white demons."

The Bishop also foresaw and foretold the suffering that awaited the Serbian people because of their sins. "The educators do not enlighten, but

[23] *Three Prayers in the Shadow of German Bayonets* was written in 1945 at our Church of St. Sava in Vienna as he was led out of the Dachau concentration camp. He wrote it on the covers of the Gospel in the altar while the German guards were standing at the doors of the church.

blind the people. They turn the children away from the Lord. They say that the Lord is but an old amulet, which their grandfathers have taken with them to their graves. What will the Lord do with them? Nothing. For they have prepared for themselves the fate of the scribes and of the Sadducees from Judea. Like them, they will listen to the rattle of the swords on their thresholds. The bald and disheveled will not dare to peep through their doors, and will die of hunger. They will be worse off than the Babylonians, the idolaters of blood and gold. There will be unimaginable starvation, wars for the plunder of food, slaughter and the burning of each other's villages, incurable diseases" (*Prayers by the Lake,* 84). He expressed himself similarly in another place: "The leaders alienate and mislead their people out of love for profit. They feed their people with lies; they instill fear in them with the injustices of the past, and embezzle for their own and for their friends' profit. What will happen to these people? Nothing. They have condemned themselves. As they behold their homes in ashes, they will flee from their country, hungry and ill, they will behold foreigners in their country and will beg them for a piece of bread, they will hear their names being cursed and will tremble ..." (*Prayers by the Lake,* 84).

Prayerful and clairvoyant, filled with uplifting evangelical love to the point of self-forgetfulness, Bishop Nikolai was a true father and shepherd of his rational flock, entrusted to him by God. He sacrificed himself wholeheartedly for his flock; he defended it from the wolves and preserved it intact. If one of his entrusted sheep left the flock and went astray on the erroneous paths of heresy or atheism, the Bishop, overcome with grief, would cry out in tears: "My heart is sick with sorrow, my Lord, and my eyes do not cease from shedding tears because many are not partaking of You, instead they seek food in the fields of hunger" (*Prayers by the Lake,* 81).

For Bishop Nikolai, the Church was his primary concern and commitment. Thus, the holy Bishop found time not only to "write and sing" but also to act. Indeed, his life was filled with manifold works and activities. In his dioceses—Ohrid-Bitolj and Zhicha—everything was evangelically renewed, regenerated and transformed. It was as if the Bishop held a pen in one hand and a hammer and a chisel in the other. He restored many churches, monasteries and monastic refectories. In his hometown of Lelich, he erected a "beautiful and glorious memorial church in which Liturgies would be sung, both in this and in the next world." Like the Apostles before him, he possessed nothing but had everything. Much wealth came into his holy hands, only to be passed on. He kept nothing for himself. Everything merely passed through him to those in need, to those in tears, and to the orphans.

The Bishop effected regeneration on the spiritual plane also. The strong impulses of his piety and his ecclesiastical life pulsed in all directions. He restored the essence of true Orthodoxy. In contrast to the Western Reformation, which was an introduction of various novelties, the emphasis here was on the return to the roots and to the original sources of Orthodox life and spirituality. This regeneration was all-inclusive, encompassing the priesthood and the people. The priestly function, pastoral care and liturgical services once again took their rightful place in the life of the Serbs. Nikolai revealed and demonstrated the dogmatic truth that "to perform the rites of the Church means to perform miracles"; although they are always present in the Church, they had become imperceptible. This was now understood not only by the priesthood, but also by the people. People began to turn to repentance, fasting, and prayer, to follow the Lord's commandments, and to attend church services. Waves of regeneration spread over the borders of the Bishop's dioceses and took hold of the whole nation.

He attracted, developed, and elevated the newly awakened religious forces in the people's soul, forces that had been crushed and had become undisciplined, untamed, and shapeless. As a result, a never-before national religious Renaissance, known as the "Christian People's Movement," emerged as a fruitful, spiritual, and evangelical event in the history of our people. Something similar may have happened in the time of St. Sava, under his holy tutelage and guidance, giving him the epithet "Teacher and Enlightener of Serbia."

This was the first time in the history of Serbia of the post-Nemanjich period[24] that the people once again embraced the Cross and the Gospel

[24] The Nemanja dynasty ruled from the late twelfth to the mid-fourteenth century. Stefan Nemanja was the founder of the medieval Serbian state and St. Sava, his youngest son, became the first Serbian Archbishop after he had successfully established the autocephaly of the national Serbian Orthodox Church. The link between state and Church remained strong throughout the rule of the Nemanja dynasty. Serbia under the rule of the Nemanja dynasty is known for its achievements in literature, architecture and painting. One of its most notable achievements is the Law Code (Zakonik) established by Tsar Dushan in 1349 and 1354. After Dushan's death in 1355 the empire gradually disintegrated, and the growing might of the Ottoman Turks led to the eventual conquest of Serbia, marked by the Battle at Kosovo Polje in 1389.—Trans.

of the Lord and rushed into the churches and monasteries as magnanimously as the ascetics and the saints in the first centuries of Christianity. Like a second St. Sava, the giant, Bishop Nikolai, stood at the head of this Christian movement of the people that brought about the Resurrection of the Cross in their souls. He poured his soul into the depths of his people and they merged into one. In this way a true miracle took place: the rebirth of the soul and the renewal of the spirit of his people.

Many of these awakened peasants, men and women alike, ignited by the divine fire, exchanged their homely dwellings for abandoned and derelict monastic refectories, which as a result led to the re-awakening and revival of our monasticism—male and female—which has always been the greatest strength and adornment of the Church.

In his work with the people, for the people, and among the people, Bishop Nikolai won over their souls, which blossomed in front of him like a bud under the sun's springtime rays of May. The people confessed their sins and weaknesses to God and awaited help and consolation from Him. In a word, the Bishop became the unique spiritual guide to all, not only to monasticism, or just to the members of the Christian movement, but also the spiritual father of the entire Serbian Orthodox nation. Many sought out his spiritual counsel both in person and in writing: priests, monks and nuns, merchants and craftsmen, officers and soldiers, workers and farmers, old and young, Serbs and Russians, and all those who had any spiritual problems, personal or national concerns.

The Bishop, an experienced spiritual father, full of divine wisdom and knowledge of life, did not spare himself in his determination and efforts to help those in doubt and trouble, and to respond to every problem and need of daily life. This resulted in the development of the unique writings of his *Missionary Letters,* which number around three hundred; these letters were novel not only in our country, but also in the Orthodox world at large. What makes these "Letters" astonishing is the fact that they possess an eternal spiritual value, although they answer concrete problems and specific questions asked by people from various walks of life. Whoever reads them discovers that he can read the letters over and over again, and will always find the answers to his own questions, the solutions to his own problems, and an incentive for zeal in his search for truth, faith, and Divine justice. Each answer of Bishop Nikolai in these "Letters" is simultaneously the answer of the Holy Orthodox Church

Fathers. There is no doubt that Nikolai was inspired by the Holy Spirit in writing the *Missionary Letters*.

The Bishop was a man of the pious Serbian people, the bone of their bones and the body of their bodies. He stood in great contrast to the Western-inclined Serbian intelligentsia of that time, which in discreet terms despised the simple people. However, the Bishop genuinely loved his people in their peasant jackets and peasant shoes; he loved the image of Christ in the people's soul. For him, the Serbian people were Christ-bearers and God-bearers and he expressed this in his prominent work *The Serbian People as a Servant of God.* The Bishop did not idealize or idolize his people. He was well acquainted with their sins and his own. He loathed the sins, just as a mother loathes the festering wounds of her beloved child. Nevertheless, Christ was and remains the treasure within every man and in every people. He gives them their permanent value, and makes them worthy of love; this is why Bishop Nikolai loved people in Christ and through Christ.

As we have seen, the Bishop loved his Serbian people passionately; he hated no one. He hated only evil and sin, whether of his own people, or of any other people. He hated "false Christianity" (see his work *The Pearl of the Coral*) that is capable of the greatest atrocities in the name of our Gentle Christ. However, he did not hate the ones who committed atrocities but rather always took pity upon them, as upon patients with fatal diseases.

Bishop Nikolai's entire life is comparable to the lives of the earlier Holy Fathers of the Church. It is therefore natural that the evangelical statements of the Holy Apostle Paul found their fulfillment in him as they did in the lives of the Holy Fathers before him: "All who desire to live godly in Christ Jesus will suffer persecution" (cf. 2 Timothy 3:12; Acts 14:22). In interpreting these words from the holy Apostle Paul, a part of the experience of the Church as well as his own, Bishop Nikolai wrote, "Can sheep live among wolves and not be attacked? Can a candle's flame remain motionless in cross draughts, and not bend to and fro? Can fruit trees grow on a high road and be left alone by a passerby? Neither can the Church of pious souls be without persecution; persecution by pagans, by idol-worshippers, by heretics, by apostates, by passions and vices, by sin and lawlessness, by the world and demons. Thus, every pious soul will suffer persecution either external or internal until it parts from the body and the world... All those that desire to live in Christ will be persecuted. The Apostle foretold this at the beginning of Christianity, and twenty centuries of Christianity clearly and loudly confirm the truth of this prophecy" (*The Prologue of Ohrid*, p. 320).

The Bishop's entire life also confirmed the truth of this prophecy. Just like in the Lives of the Saints: "The devil, not able to withstand such a life full of virtues, and not able to watch the Apostle turn more and more people away from him, leading them to God, aroused some evil people against him so as to do him harm." And indeed, Nikolai was never free of opponents and enemies either. Because of his "pious and holy life," he was never free from some form of persecution. At the height of his work for the good of his people, the devil always stirred up someone to attack and slander the one who pleased God, particularly during the time of his struggle against the Concordat, which was soon followed by the inhuman occupation. The Bishop suffered violent and brutal persecution in prisons, in exile, and in jails and concentration camps by the occupying power which, like a blind weapon of the devil, inflicted upon him great cruelty and suffering. The sufferings of this great Preacher, Confessor, and Ascetic of the Gospel continued into the final years of his life, which he spent in exile, in a foreign land where his requiem was held.

But this co-sufferer of Christ "for the sake of justice" never became discouraged, never abated, and never wavered in his belief in the "final victory of good." At the end of his life, he could boldly repeat the Apostle's words: *I have fought a good fight, I have finished my course, I have kept the faith* (2 Timothy 4:7).

The pious Serbian people loved their Bishop during his lifetime, loved him even more during persecutions and exile, and loved him the most after his death. And as more time passes, the greater is the love. The Bishop has always been and remained "a rule of faith and an example of meekness." This is the reason for the people's great thirst for the Bishop, for his books, and his works.

In the consciousness of the Orthodox people, he was already a saint in his lifetime. Without a doubt, he remains a saint after his death, too. The first to address him and to pray to him as a saint was Fr. Justin Popovich. While still living here on earth, and after his repose, he always called him the "Holy Bishop Nikolai." Whether he gave a sermon at the memorial service—held each year at the Bishop's memorial church in his hometown Lelich —or whether he wrote about him, or spoke about him, he always said: the "Holy Bishop Nikolai."

The Orthodox people presently pray to Bishop Nikolai in their afflictions and illnesses with their petitions for help; they receive consolation, relief, and healing according to their faith and according to their love for Christ. We believe and hope that the glory of Holy Bishop Nikolai will be revealed by a public divine celebration,[25] and await even greater blessings from the Bishop than those received during his lifetime.

The Translation of the Relics of the Holy Hierarch Nikolai

When man sets out to work he needs a certain amount of preparation beforehand, the greater the work, the greater the preparation. The translation of a saint's relics from one place to another is an enormous undertaking for the Church and the people; this is why necessary preparations take a long time. Saints do not travel unless there is a great need. The preparations, that is, the essential and fundamental preparations for the translation of holy Bishop Nikolai's relics began at the moment of his blessed repose in the Lord. The logistics followed as a consequence of these preparations and their modifications.

Indeed, on March 18, 1956, at the time of holy Bishop Nikolai's repose, a significant change had begun to take place. In his feelings, his inexhaustible love and concern, his thoughts and ideas, as well as his actions and efforts, the Bishop was more in Serbia than in America during his years of exile. In his body he was in America, but his holy soul was in Serbia, calling on and visiting Zhicha, Studenica, St. Naum by the Lake of Ohrid, and his hometown Lelich. Till his last breath he suffered from an unbearable nostalgia for his *Domaj*,[26] for his suffering Serbia, martyred and crucified on the Cross. This nostalgia for his homeland, which was his cross and the expression of his unquenchable love, tormented him and wore him down like a treacherous disease. The fire of this love gradually consumed him.

But after the Bishop had forever shut his eyes, the eyes of his mind, and the eyes of his much weeping soul, something completely unexpected happened; a deep-seated nostalgia for Bishop Nikolai began to torment Serbia. Serbia was left desiring him, just as he had desired her. As

[25] Bishop Nikolai was formally glorified by the Serbian Orthodox Church on May 19, 2003.

[26] *Domaj:* an endearing term for home.—Trans.

time passed, this nostalgia gained impetus, becoming harder to bear. Even though masses of people attended the yearly memorial services in his hometown of Lelich, this did not diminish the longing for him. These services were just like drops of fresh water in the burning desert. Serbia waited in hope and longed for the day when she would finally welcome back Bishop Nikolai from the cold and distant foreign land of America, and embrace him as a mother in her wounded bosom.

This yearning of the true Serbia, the Serbia of St. Sava, grew stronger in response to Nikolai's fiercest enemies and opponents. As the godless communist regime with its cronies—unfortunately, some of them from the Serbian ranks too—attacked Bishop Nikolai and his works with increasing ruthlessness, so did the love of the pious people grow towards him. The regime, in fact, did not spare "epithets" via its controlled press and other media outlets in its attempt to stain and malign the holy Bishop in the eyes of the people, especially the youth. He was denounced as a heretic, a reactionary, a mason, an English agent, a German agent, and a collaborator. The regime went as far as to proclaim him an enemy of the people. However, the people had their own measuring rod and a "sixth sense," and came to their own unmistakable conclusion, namely, that whomever the atheists and communists attacked must be good and have some significance. So, all the attempts to "demonize" Bishop Nikolai produced the opposite effect in the soul of the people. Nikolai gradually emerged as a contemporary Serbian saint.

Although the holy grave of beloved Nikolai was far away in both space and time, he was a living presence in the consciousness of the Serbian people. They whispered, sang, and talked about him. He was especially dear to the Serbian monks and nuns, and to his faithful "Bogomoljci." Their memories of Nikolai were alive and their love for him was boundless. The spiritual songs of Bishop Nikolai contributed a lot; they were sung at every occasion and at every gathering of the "Bogomoljci," particularly at the celebrations of the monasteries' patron saints, events reminiscent of the former gatherings of the Bogomoljci that Bishop Nikolai had once organized and led.

The already-mentioned annual memorial services for Bishop Nikolai played an important role in preserving and rekindling his loving memory. In his hometown of Lelich, the nuns of the nearby monastery of Chelije conscientiously saw to their preparations with great love. The holy Elder of Chelije, Fr. Justin was the main source of inspiration at these memorial services and remained so until his death. Fr. Justin painted the first icon, not made by hands, of holy Bishop Nikolai in the souls of the pious Serbian faithful with his prayers and especially his sermons; an icon of the Serbian Evangelist, Serbian Apostle, Serbian Confessor, Serbian Martyr, Serbian Prophet...

Soon, many people were praying to holy Bishop Nikolai, asking for help and protection in times of trouble, temptations, and illnesses. Their pleas were frequently answered. Although not properly recorded yet, many testimonies exist of the personal experiences of honest people, descriptions of the wondrous and grace-filled help from holy Bishop Nikolai to them and their relatives. The epithet "Holy Bishop Nikolai" was spontaneous and had spread among the laypeople, the monks and nuns, and the clergy. The time was ripe for the formal glorification of the Saint. Our Russian brethren in America had already proclaimed him a Saint and had icons of holy Bishop Nikolai; his sanctity was first felt and expressed in colors by the deeply Orthodox Russian soul.

The current atmosphere here in Serbia is gradually changing, too. The Broz nightmare[27] is beginning to relent. One can breathe, think and speak more freely. The present ardent spreading and rekindling of Bishop Nikolai's cult is greatly attributed to the *Voice of the Church*, a newly established journal for Christian culture and Church life, published by the clergy of the Diocese of Shabac-Valjevo. It is noteworthy that the *Voice of the Church* has chosen Bishop Nikolai as its patron and celebrates him as its "Patron Saint."

So, what was meant to happen and what many awaited with hope finally did happen. On March 18, 1987, two eminent Serbian bishops, Jovan of the Diocese of Shabac-Valjevo and Amphilochius of the Diocese of Vrshac-Banat, celebrated the Divine Liturgy in memory of holy Bishop Nikolai. A great number of the faithful and monks and nuns participated in the Liturgy, which was concelebrated by the clergy at the Cathedral in Shabac. The troparion and kontakion of the saint were chanted on this occasion. At the end of the Divine Liturgy, the *slavski kolach*[28] was offered, which had been prepared by the *Voice of the Church* to honor the

[27] Refers to the communist regime of Josip Broz Tito.—TRANS.

[28] *Slavski kolach:* an offering of specially prepared bread for the celebration of a patron saint.—TRANS.

new Serbian and all-Orthodox Saint Nikolai. The spiritual joy and enthusiasm on this occasion was great.

On this festive occasion, the sisters of the of Chelije Monastery presented their beautifully hand-painted icon of the holy Bishop. Copies of the icon were subsequently published and made accessible to the people at large. The icon corners of many Serbian homes were enriched with this new icon. One more Saint and powerful intercessor was now standing before the Throne of Almighty God.

Unfortunately, certain "hard liners" used this celebration for a renewed attack on Bishop Nikolai and on those devoted to him. Even certain individuals from within the Church who held a grudge against Bishop Jovan and especially against the "Justinians"[29]criticized them for performing the glorification rite of Bishop Nikolai ahead of the "formal Church." At the following year's celebration of the Patron Saint, Bishop Jovan responded to the criticism in person. He said the following: "The Church has never made proclamations of saints ahead of the people. In fact, it is the other way around. The people proclaim someone as a saint first, and the Church follows with an official acknowledgment later... Therefore, we now stand in front of the people who venerate Nikolai as a saint, but we are not imposing his sanctity on anyone... He is venerated as a saint by the people at large, which is the first phase of sainthood. We are stating this today because we have been criticized for prematurely proclaiming Bishop Nikolai a saint. There is nothing premature about this. The respective phases of the glorification of saints as prescribed by our Church from time immemorial are proceeding accordingly" (*Voice of the Church*, February 1991, p. 22).

These "attacks" and "criticisms" were not able to hinder the spread of the cult of Bishop Nikolai among the people, or lessen the yearning for holy Bishop Nikolai's return from exile, where he had spent the past fifty years of his life and repose. Prominent Serbs in literary and intellectual circles shared these sentiments of the faithful masses.

On March 25, 1989, the third anniversary of the celebration of the Patron Saint of the *Voice of the Church* at the Spiritual Academy at Lelich, our distinguished and bold writer Vuk Drashkovich delivered a speech about Bishop Nikolai, saying, "In the hope that Serbia has been freed

[29] Followers of Fr. Justin.—TRANS.

from pharaoh's bondage, I join the call for Bishop and holy Nikolai Velimirovich to be issued a PASSPORT." For, "Serbia can show herself free of her shackles only when Saint Nikolai has a passport..." As expected, the Academy, Vuk Drashkovich, and the *Voice of the Church,* which first printed this speech in February 1989, were bitterly attacked by the one-man regime. However, nowadays, these attacks receive little attention.

The people's desire for the rapid return of Bishop Nikolai gradually took on a more concrete form. The new head of the Serbian Orthodox Church, His Holiness Patriarch Pavle—a man of prayer, an ascetic, and a struggler—together with the summit of the SPC[30] took a positive and concrete step toward the translation of the relics of holy Bishop Nikolai. At their regular meeting in May of 1990, the Holy Hierarchical Synod adopted the suggestions and view of His Grace Lavrentije, Bishop of Shabac-Valjevo and passed the following historical resolution: "Their Graces, Stefan, Bishop of Zhicha, Lavrentius, Bishop of Shabac-Valjevo, Christopher, Bishop of Eastern America, and Mitrofan, Bishop of Toplica and the Acting Bishop of Midwestern America, have been requested to organize the translation of the relics of Nikolai, Bishop of Zhicha of blessed repose, from the monastery of St. Sava in Libertyville to his hometown and memorial in Lelich."

Following this decision, the Holy Hierarchical Synod formed a commission to direct and carry out its resolution. However, the preparations were conducted with little public disclosure. It was only in the spring of 1991 that the wider public was officially informed of the translation of Bishop Nikolai's relics.

In addition to these formal steps of the SPC, Bishop Nikolai's nephew, a retired Supreme Court judge and his only living relative,[31] was also involved with the translation of his relics and was thus able to carry out his duty as a relative toward his great uncle. He also fulfilled the wish and testament of his cousin, His Grace Jovan, the Bishop of Shabac-Valjevo of blessed repose, who had long desired for the holy Bishop to be brought from America much earlier. Bishop Jovan, however, did not witness this event in his lifetime.

[30] Acronym for "Srpksa Pravoslavna Crkva," i.e., the Serbian Orthodox Church.—TRANS.

[31] According to the wondrous Providence of God, he passed away on the same morning (May 12) that Bishop Nikolai arrived at Lelich.

As the preparations neared their end, Nikolai's Serbia and Lelich were finally ready for the great day. The relics of Bishop Nikolai were taken from the tomb of the monastery of St. Sava in Libertyville where they had been laid to rest for thirty-five years, and were now placed in the casket for their journey. A solemn church service in Libertyville followed. Serbs from America and Canada accompanied St. Nikolai with dignity and great sorrow because of their parting. Young and old Serbs alike, with whom holy "Deka"—as he had been called long ago—had shared the good and bad during his exile of nearly half-a-century, surrounded him. His casket was covered with the Serbian Tri-color flag. They kissed his cross and said their good-byes with their last farewell prayers. This was their final farewell to St. Nikolai whose relics were about to usher in a new era of St. Sava's legacy and unity for the Serbian people. At the end of this moving occasion, our prominent writer Antonije Djurich delivered a brilliant and very warm speech about St. Nikolai.

Unfortunately, Nikolai's welcome in Serbia fell short of all expectations and was far from what the Bishop deserved. Insufficient dissemination of information and the continued fear of the "popular" regime may have been responsible, or maybe the hardened hearts and dulled minds from the winter of half a century of communism, a winter that refused to give way to the approaching Serbian spring. Whatever the reason, the welcome at the Belgrade Surchin airport was very disheartening. Altogether, there were four to five hundred souls, including the clergy, monks and nuns, who were mainly from the Diocese of Shabac-Valjevo. However, for those present, this encounter, which had been fifty years in the making and which had followed the violent separation of Bishop Nikolai from his native soil, was a very moving experience.

The welcome in front of the Church of St. Sava on the hill of Vrachar was more encouraging. Two to three thousand people were present, a number small in comparison to over a million Serbs in Belgrade! In Zhicha, which Bishop Nikolai had restored and whose second patron he had become, there were barely over a thousand souls, mainly Bogomoljci and monastics who had gathered for his welcome on May 5. Nevertheless, the relics remained at Zhicha until May 12, so that groups of faithful with their priests from various locations could pay their respects.

It was only when the Bishop arrived in his small village of Lelich on May 12 that his welcome was really magnificent: thirty thousand people from all around Serbia had gathered there. But this too, strictly speaking, was insignificant in comparison to what Bishop Nikolai deserved and to the extent the Serbian people were indebted to him. Even so, the sight was very moving, satisfying both the eyes and the soul. The entire Hierarchical Synod, with Patriarch Pavle at its head and a large number of clergy, concelebrated the Divine Liturgy, which was held outside on a platform erected for the occasion. The service was beautiful. The people showed great devotion and were delighted with this great gift from the heavenly Serbia.

Divine Liturgies were held everywhere the relics of the holy Bishop were taken (Belgrade, Zhicha and Lelich) and was followed by Academic symposiums. Our well-known spiritual fathers, writers, and other academic people delivered lectures at these gatherings. In their speeches they described his greatness and discussed his works, depicting the attributes of Bishop Nikolai's holy image in most beautiful colors.[32]

The Veneration of Bishop Nikolai

Following their arrival in Serbia from America, Bishop Nikolai's holy relics became the object of devotion and veneration, and Lelich, a new place of pilgrimage. At Surchin airport, the head of the Serbian Orthodox Church, His Holiness Patriarch Pavle, together with other hierarchs, the clergy and monastics, venerated the reliquary containing the relics. Crowds of people approached the reliquary and venerated the new Saint's relics in the churches of St. Sava in Belgrade, in Zhicha and at Lelich. After May 12, particularly on Sundays and holidays during the summer months, individuals and groups of Serbian Orthodox people came to Lelich to venerate their spiritual shepherd.

The majority of pilgrims always took the opportunity to visit the nearby Chelije Monastery and venerate the grave of our second great modern luminary and Saint, the venerable Fr. Justin. So, Nikolai and Justin, as well as Lelich and Chelije, have imprinted themselves in the consciousness of the people as names that will always go together. Hence, Lelich has become for Serbia (and we hope it will remain so) what Ostrog [St. Basil] is for Montenegro, what St. Sergius of Radonezh is for Russia, St. John of Rila is for Bulgaria, and St. Nectarios of Aegina is for Greece.

[32] The speeches are published in their entirety in *Glas Crkve,* March 1991.

People offer their prayers to Bishop Nikolai for the sick and for other afflicted souls. Parakleses and troparia are read over his relics, which have been clothed in new hierarchical vestments and placed into a new reliquary.[33] The holy Bishop accepts every prayerful request and presents them all with great boldness before our All-merciful heavenly Father and Lover of mankind.

Without a doubt, the holy Bishop is kneeling together with St. Sava and the other Serbian saints before the throne of the Creator, asking for mercy and help in our times of trouble and suffering, befallen us once again because of our sins. We firmly believe and hope that God will answer their prayers and forgive the Serbs their sins. And the Serbs will finally turn to God again, to their only Friend and Savior.

The holy Bishop has taken a long time to return to us, and when he came, he did not come empty-handed. He showered us richly with many gifts. His arrival to Serbia has brought many blessings. While still in America, as the Serbs bid farewell to their beloved shepherd, God poured out His great mercy upon the Serbs in America who had been divided, and lived in dissension and discord.[34] On that day they all gathered together around the reliquary, experienced the same emotions, and prayed together for the same things. They entreated God to grant them the Bishop's most fervent prayer: "O Lord, help the Serbs to unite, to multiply and to become godly." As the sun shone upon the monastery of St. Sava and the people spread out into the park and onto the sidewalks as they arrived from all directions, the following public announcement from the Holy Hierarchical Synod in Belgrade became known: "In the spirit of brotherly love and evangelical conscientiousness towards the reestablishment of the unity of our Church and people in the tradition of St. Sava, the fundamental issues which endanger this unity in the United States of America, Canada, Australia, and Western Europe have been examined. We pray to our God, Christ the Unifier of mankind and the only Head

[33] The washing and vesting were conducted on October 16–17, 1991, by His Grace Artemije, Bishop of Rashka-Prizren and assisted by Protosygel Jovan Radosavljevich (also from Lelich), a monk from the monastery of Crna Reka, and a nun from Chelije Monastery.

[34] The Serbian Orthodox Church suffered a schism, which divided the Church between the Serbian Orthodox Church with the Patriarchate in Belgrade, Serbia and the "Free Serbian Orthodox Church" abroad. This schism lasted almost thirty years, from 1963 to 1992, when Patriarch Pavle, together with the Holy Synod, finally reached reconciliation.

of the Orthodox Church to heal all the wounds of our spiritual and national body and being, in order to reach an all-embracing reconciliation." The scene following this general announcement was very moving. Serbs from both sides of this terrible schism were now standing together around St. Nikolai, asking forgiveness from each other in front of his holy relics. A full reconciliation begun this way, rekindled by the warm prayers of the holy Bishop, was reached in less than a year, on the feast of the Meeting of the Lord at the Cathedral in Belgrade. On that day His Holiness Patriarch Pavle concelebrated the Divine Liturgy with Metropolitan Irinej of the New Grachanica Metropolitanate of America and with a large number of bishops, clergy and the faithful. Without a doubt, holy Bishop Nikolai helped heal the severe wound of the living organism of the Serbian Orthodox Church and Serbian people, which had been bleeding for twenty-nine years.

We hope our holy Bishop will continue to keep watch over us and pray for us. A young Serbia will rise around his holy relics, brought up on the ideals of St. Sava, in the tradition of Kosovo and King Lazar. Then freedom and victory will finally dawn upon the Serbian people.

Epilogue by Hieromonk Athanasius (Yevtich)[35]

Since this publication of Fr. Artemije (Radosavljevich)[36] of Lelich, Abbot of Crna Reka, who has so far expounded the works and the person of Bishop Nikolai of Ohrid and Zhicha, I have found it necessary to supplement the book with some additional information.

Fr. Artemije has not dealt with the numerous attacks against Nikolai and his works; and neither did Bishop Nikolai for that matter. Attacks against him began at the very start of his public life, lasted until his death, and continue to this day. Thirty years after his repose, it is high time to calmly and objectively discuss some of the criticisms, accusations and defamations against the person and works of Nikolai Velimirovich.

Without a doubt, he was an unusual and a complex man, and for some, a controversial figure of our times. There are many who stumbled over him, over his works, and over his actions, primarily because of judgmentalism and ignorance. They declared him a "heretic," a "reactionary,"

[35] Currently retired Bishop of Hercegovina.—Trans.

[36] Currently retired Bishop of Rashka-Prizren and Kosovo-Metohije.—Ed.

a "Mason," an "English" or else a "German agent," and a "collaborator," the "enemy of the state," a "clerical nationalist," etc. Nikolai was none of these, and this is why he never defended himself or "justified" himself to anyone. He revealed his inner peace and Christian forgiveness for his slanderers in what he himself on many occasions called "the love of Christ, the love of man, and the love of patriotism."

These words, that is, the love of Christ, the love of man, and the love of patriotism, were spoken and written down in his *Textbook on Saint Sava*, published in 1935. In the same year of the anniversary of St. Sava,[37] he delivered his renowned lecture "On the Nationalism of St. Sava" at Kolarac (printed separately in 1935). In this talk, Nikolai spoke about St. Sava's "love of God, love of man, and love of patriotism." This lecture exists to the present-day and is accessible to anyone who wants to know for himself what Nikolai had then said and with what intention. However, this lecture has lately become the occasion for certain renewed attacks against Nikolai. Namely, in more recent times, since the war,[38] an insane campaign against Nikolai, against his name and his works, is being promoted because of certain words in this lecture. In this lecture of 1935, Nikolai's mention of the national work of the "Leader of the German Reich" has been construed as "praise" for the latter who, as Nikolai stated, "in the past two years (that is, from 1933 to 1935) has succeeded to a certain extent in organizing the Protestant segment of the population into a resemblance of a national Church," something which St. Sava had in fact already accomplished a long time ago for the Serbs. Nikolai praised the "present German leader" (he did not mention Hitler's name) who "as a layperson of the twentieth century, had arrived at the same idea as St. Sava, to undertake the most important work for his people," that is, the creation of a national Church, which is an act "that befits only a saint, a genius or a hero," as St. Sava himself was. We repeat: Nikolai said this in 1935. One may admit that he was quick in word and with his pen at times, and that maybe even these words were not thought through well enough or carefully worded. However, at the time these words were not understood as an actual praise of the yet-to-be public manifestation of Hitler's criminal Nazism in Europe; nor did these words offend anyone in particular; neither

[37] The seven hundredth anniversary of St. Sava's repose.—Ed.

[38] The author most probably is referring to World War II.—Trans.

did Nikolai ever repeat them again. On the contrary, as we shall see further on, soon afterwards, he criticized and condemned Hitler and his totalitarianism, under which he and his people also suffered bitterly in the ensuing war. (In contrast to this criticism, the first socialist country in the world and its "charismatic" Leader, as well as numerous satellite states, praised Hitler and were his allies for many years, up to June 22, 1941, and even welcomed the Führer's conquest of Poland and Paris).[39]

To our knowledge, the first defamation of Nikolai's unsuccessful comparison in 1935 was not made until 1945 by the "priest" Nikola Drenovac (printed in the journal *Slobodna Rech* in America). The accusation was subsequently repeated frequently in our homeland, whenever it was expedient to accuse Nikolai and furthermore to "prove" a real or an imaginary "fault" of his. This was the main source from which Nikolai's alleged "pro-Hitler" position was drawn, and his alleged subsequent "collaboration." Nevertheless, by the same logic, Nikolai's arrest by the Germans as early as July 12, 1941, followed by his internment and imprisonment in Dachau, poses a serious problem to this thinking. His internment in Dachau, however, has been suppressed recently as an unimportant "detail" or interpreted as "some strange plans" the Germans allegedly had with Nikolai and with the Serbian Patriarch Gavrilo. The Germans were well aware of the patriotic position of both men, demonstrated on March 27, and of their refusal to collaborate or make any public announcements to the advantage of the Reich and its Leader. This was sealed by the blood of Nikolai's Kraljevo, Milanovac, and Zhicha, and of Patriarch Gavrilo's Kragujevac and Belgrade, as well as by the entire Serbian Church and Yugoslav homeland.

In answer to the accusation of the defrocked priest, Nikola Drenovac, Nikolai wrote the following letter to the Serbian Bishop of America, Dionysius, dated February 20, 1946: "In relation to the accusation directed at me from the 'fellow priest' in *Slobodna Rech,* you should know the truth, and I do not wish to enter into polemics. And the truth is this: I delivered

[39] For the sake of complete information let us be reminded of one other incident, equally misconstrued: Sometime around 1935, as the Bishop of Bitolj, Nikolai took up the restoration of a military cemetery and in the process he also restored the cemetery of German soldiers killed in World War I. (He said, "A dead soldier is no longer an enemy to a Serb.") As Hitler learned about this, he had a medal cross for "civilian merits" awarded to him through his diplomatic representative. Nikolai never mentioned this cross, or took advantage of it even at the time when he was arrested, interrogated, and imprisoned by the Germans.

a lecture at the University of Kolarchevo about the nationalism of St. Sava, on the anniversary of St. Sava in 1935, and whoever is not acquainted with it would think that I mentioned the leader of the German people during the war. In the latter instance, why would the Germans then imprison me from the first day to the last? At the time, I was exalting St. Sava and not Hitler. I had said that St. Sava, the saint, the genius and the hero of the Serbian people, had created the Serbian national Church seven hundred years ago and had united the entire Serbian people into one Church, a deed which was not repeated in the West. I said that Pascal had later made an attempt to create a national Gallic Church for the French in the seventeenth century but had failed. Whereas, a leader of the German people, a simple craftsman, was presently attempting to create a national Church in the twentieth century, that is, he was trying to accomplish that which befits only a saint, a genius, and a hero: St. Sava. In a later talk (or article, I cannot recall), I once again turned to Hitler's attempt at the creation of a united national German Church and I quoted his words at the Reichstag: 'I have tried,' he said, 'to unite the German churches into one national German Church but my attempt has failed.' Consequently, everything said and written in 1935 that was associated with our celebration was said as a eulogy to St. Sava, the saint, the genius, and the hero, and not to anyone else. Both Pascal and Hitler served only as examples of failures in comparison to the brilliant success of St. Sava. Whoever has ears let him hear and whoever has a mind with which to comprehend let him understand." (This letter of Nikolai was published in the American press several times.)

Next to this crystal clear answer and explanation of Nikolai's lecture from 1935, we will introduce two other texts dated after 1935, before Hitler's invasions and his bloody establishment of the "new order" in Europe. On New Year's Day of 1939, in his sermon with the characteristic title of "In the Shadow of Iron and Smoke," Nikolai said: "We are living in the shadow of iron and smoke, in the darkness and shadow of death. In 1939 war costs will increase by the billions in all countries, and the number of murderous war machines will increase... Yet, in contrast to all this madness, the human race believes in the good, and hopes in the good" (*Zichki Blagovestnik,* no. 1, 1939, 4–9).

Later, in April of 1939, Nikolai published the following text about "The Three Reichs": "In the West there is a desire for a western kingdom: for a great Reich. The first Reich was founded by Napoleon. This Reich (western kingdom) lasted for eight years and then it collapsed and fell into ruins. The French created this first Reich. The second Reich was established half a century after the fall of the first one. This second Reich (second western kingdom) was established under the leadership of Prussia and Austria and their ally, Italy, in the hope of gaining the title deed to this kingdom in World War I, which already bore its new name. This kingdom was supposed to be called 'Middle Europe'; however, to our relief and to their misfortune it remained only an idea, a utopia. The first Reich provoked a world war and its instigators perished. The second Reich provoked a world war and once again its instigators perished. Currently, a third Reich under the leadership of Germany, Italy, and Japan is being established. This one, too, will provoke a world war. However, the fate, which awaits this third Reich has already been demonstrated by the first two. It is like those who have great plans but are unaware of their impending death" (*Zichki Blagovesnik,* April 1939, inside cover).

Any commentary is redundant here. However, the German commentary prompted the arrest of Nikolai and his detention at Ljubostinja (where he personally protested against the Germans and the massive deaths inflicted by their firing squads in Kraljevo in October: "Is it possible that this is German culture: that for every German, one hundred innocent Serbs are killed! Even the Turks were more just... If I am guilty, kill me. I would much rather die than watch the daily sufferings of my people"). Thereafter, he was placed under house arrest in Vojlovica together with Patriarch Gavrilo and later they were both transferred to the concentration camp of Dachau. They were imprisoned there from September 1944 to the end of January in 1945, and both fell ill. Afterwards, not by their own wishes, but by the order of others, they were taken by German guards first to Vienna in January and then all over Austria, Slovenia, and Italy in April; and they were escorted everywhere. Getting Patriarch Gavrilo and Nikolai out of Dachau was made possible through the intervention of Ljotich[40] and Nedich,[41] who at the time were evidently holding

[40] Dimitrije Ljotich (1891–1945), Minister of Justice, 1931; Commanding General Officer of Serbian Volunteer Corps, 1941–1944; killed in a car crash, 1945.—Trans.

[41] Milan Nedich (1877–1946), Chief of the General Staff of the Yugoslav Army, Minister of War in the Royal Yugoslav Government, Prime Minister in the government called Government of National Salvation in the German-occupied Serbia, 1941–1944.—Trans.

onto the authority of these unstained Serbian spiritual giants in the hope of obtaining some help or exoneration from the imminent arrival of the Western Allies. By then, Hitler, and everything under him, was undeniably collapsing. In those days, in April of 1945, Nikolai and the Patriarch were taken to the military refugee camps in Istria, in parts of Slovenia and Italy, where the remainder of the soldiers under Ljotich, Djujich,[42] and Jevdjevich[43] were. Apart from conducting church services on the occasion of the feast of St. Sava in Vienna and on Pascha at other places (earlier they had conducted church services in Vojlovica and toward the end also in Dachau), there is no evidence of Nikolai or Gavrilo having said anything in favor of Hitler or anything against their homeland and people. It is true that Nikolai delivered a sermon at the funeral of Dimitrije Ljotich, who had died in a car accident, a sermon to an Orthodox faithful (the latter had tried to associate himself with Nikolai earlier although Nikolai rejected the notion of being a "Ljotichevac"). As usual, Nikolai delivered an oral sermon and, therefore, the "text" published in 1949 as his speech to Ljotich is not authentic as far as we are concerned. Even if this text may contain some of Nikolai's thoughts and expressions, those are matters that relate only to his own "political positions and choices," "weaknesses in his ideas," that is, "faults" from which no one in the history of man is exempt. The sermon can also be understood, to a certain extent, as his repayment to Ljotich for having extracted him out of the hell of Dachau. In any case, there is no justification or reason for the malicious defamation as a "war criminal" of this afflicted person, an accusation which has been repeated on various occasions in our homeland, both verbally, at different gatherings and written in the press.[44]

Only recently has a more sober and responsible approach been taken regarding this matter (i.e., in the journal of the Serbian SUP[45] *Bezbednost*, no. 5, 1982, p. 417, remark 19), exemplified in the following: "How much

[42] Momchilo R. Djujich (1907–1999), in allegiance to King Peter II of Yugoslavia; Commander of the Dinara Chetnik Division, 1941–1944 (Chetnik derives from the word cheta, i.e., military detachment, division; denoting those belonging to one).—Trans.

[43] Dobroslav Jevdjevich (1895–1962), Commander of the Chetnik Corps in Lika-Kordun and the Coast, 1944–1945.—Trans.

[44] We remind the readers of the article "Whom Does Egalitarianism Serve?" printed in the Journal *Pravoslavlje* of August 1981, which was written in answer to the slanderous claim of Nikolai as a "war criminal."

[45] SUP: the Ministry of Internal Affairs, i.e., Police Department.—Trans.

political damage is created through unconfirmed information and qualifications is clearly evident in the example of the frequent labeling of Bishop Nikolai as a war criminal. He has actually never been declared a war criminal and therefore, there is no reason for us to attach this label to his name. His opposition to the NOR[46] and to the socialist Yugoslavia can be proven with a series of other, undisputed, and equally "sound" data and qualifications such as: a sympathizer of the Chetnik and Ljotich movement, a political emigrant, a clerical nationalist etc.," P. Ilich writes.

In relation to these last "qualifications" of Nikolai, we are compelled to publicly proclaim, in regard to Nikolai's thirtieth anniversary, that first, we believe it makes no sense to defend Nikolai from "clerical nationalism" ascribed to him here and elsewhere, simply because this purely political slogan is attributed to all of us who are Orthodox by the well-known Yugoslav "egalitarians." Nikolai was and has remained an outspoken opponent of clericalism and related clerical nationalism (for example, see his open letter to Koroshec of 1937). With regard to the other accusations, we shall say the following: Nikolai was without a doubt an opponent of the Germans; he opposed their ideology and their bloody occupation, as well as any kind of "collaboration" with them. (Had he even desired any "collaboration," the Germans would not have believed him because of his participation in March 27; even without that, they considered him an "Englishman.") The German treatment of him from the beginning to the end of the war is, in itself, evidence enough. As a clearly freethinking son of his people and a renowned fighter for freedom and unification in earlier years, he was also certainly in favor of the liberation of his people and their homeland at this time. The Germans knew this well and were always afraid of his influence on the Serbian people. (Even before Nikolai's arrest, the German command had sent two German Protestant pastors to Zhicha with the instruction to tell him that since the "Serbian people listen to him," he should exert his influence on them not to rebel and create difficulties for themselves. Nikolai answered them, "The Serbian people do not listen to me because, had they listened, you would not be here.") The Germans were particularly afraid of his influence on armed dissenters, especially the Chetniks, and so they had him quickly removed from Zhicha, which they then bombarded heavily, ransacked and destroyed. Because of the continued fear of his influence on the Chetniks,

[46] NOR: the War of National Liberation (i.e. Communist takeover).—TRANS.

he was removed from Ljubostinja and placed in Banat, and later in Dachau where the Germans felt more secure.[47] (It is said that a number of letters from Nikolai are still in existence from the time of his internment and imprisonment. We are certain that all his letters are of a spiritual nature, have a Christian content, and are in no way compromising. In expectation of their publication, if they exist, we are presenting a short letter written to his mother that we have obtained; a letter written in pencil on a piece of paper folded many times. It is dated September 2/15, 1943, and was written in Vojlovica: "I kiss the hands of my dear Mother; I bless and send her my greetings. We received everything you have sent to us so far. We are very grateful. You write that you pray to God and that Priest Djoka serves and delivers sermons in church regularly. That is the way it should be. *All our hope is in our Lord God.*[48] And all the people need to repent of their sins, from stealing, quarrels and lawsuits, and should pray to God for forgiveness and mercy. Regards to Pelagija and to the others....")

Here, we shall introduce an important text by Nikolai, from the time of his imprisonment with Patriarch Gavrilo in Vojlovica (where Nikolai also wrote the Paraklesis to the Most Holy Mother of God "Slovesnica," written in his characteristic manner around Christmas of 1943: "Bless, O Mother of God, brethren, forgive me a sinner—*captive in prison, free in Christ*" (italics by the author). This unpublished and little known document which has been preserved to this day clearly shows the position of Bishop Nikolai and Patriarch Gavrilo toward the NOR, which continues to be of interest to us. Namely, on December 18 and 21, 1943, Milan Nedich arrived at the Vojlovac Monastery escorted by the German Captain Meier, the Chief of the Gestapo Department of Religion in Belgrade. According to German instructions, Nedich requested the Patriarch to return to Belgrade, call an Assembly of the Hierarchs of the Serbian Church and issue a joint proclamation against the Communist Party and the Partisans. In return, the Patriarch would be reinstated to his Patriarchal Throne in Belgrade; Nikolai would be permitted "to come and stay only in the Pa-

[47] In the "Collection of Documents and Data on the NOR," published by the Institute of Military History in Belgrade, 1981, vol. 14, book 1, p.129, a Chetnik document published under no. 46, dated January 1, 1942, provides evidence of the German apprehension with regard to Nikolai's influence on the Chetniks and of his imminent internment in Vojlovica.

[48] Emphasis placed by Bishop Athanasius (Yevtich).—TRANS.

triarchate without the right to return to his diocese in Zhicha." Meier denied the Patriarch's initial request for a consultation with Nikolai because allegedly the former did not have permission to talk with Nikolai. However, Patriarch Gavrilo's request for a few more days to respond was granted. According to the Patriarch's wish, his answer was written by Nikolai. The Bishop of Shabac, Jovan, who spent his entire internment in Vojlovica, has safeguarded this letter to the present-day, that is, the written answer to Milan Nedich, which was addressed to him by his earlier title, "General and Minister" rather than "President" in order to avoid a formal recognition of his change in status. The letter is as follows:

> A man who has been imprisoned for the past thirty two months, stripped of his freedom and of his rights, deprived of all forms of communication with the outside world, unable to follow public events and the stormy events of our contemporary times, who cannot exert his free will or pursue any undisturbed activity from prison, as is the case with me, is, therefore, not competent to communicate in public or to carry the responsibility of public affairs [underlined in the original version]. However, I can state my personal opinion and my firm conviction that the Serbian Orthodox Church has always been, is, and will always most decisively be opposed to every destructive actof atheistic fury against the Serbian people with the intention to destroy them morally and physically.[49]

Further on in this text, he asserted that the Serbian Orthodox Church was ready to help

> your efforts [i.e., Nedich's] and the efforts of all patriotic Serbs, for the protection and salvation of the pious Serbian people. With God's help, the Serbian Orthodox Church will be able to fully take up both tasks only after Her undisturbed, rightful and canonically legal functioning has been restored, which was cut short two and a half years ago.

[49] Witnesses have testified that Nikolai made a later comment about this last sentence and that it related to the German and to the atheistic Soviet attacks to the same extent; the quoted text is open for such an interpretation.

This text was the joint answer of the Patriarch and Nikolai. The result was their continued imprisonment and soon thereafter they were taken to the concentration camp of Dachau. One should provide some additional information and explanation here. Namely, it was on that same occasion that Nikolai told Patriarch Gavrilo that "a proclamation against the Communist Party would have been a grave mistake and an unpardonable error," because, "it is very dangerous for the Church to issue proclamations against a political party, in this case the Communist Party. The Church is not concerned with parties and party programs. The Church is only concerned with whether a respective party propagates atheism or not. We are against atheism whether it is from the left or right; in other words, we are opposed to Hitler's atheists just as we are opposed to the Soviet ones. We can issue a proclamation only in so far as it opposes atheism and not Communists. For should Communism recognize religion and revoke atheism from its party's program tomorrow, which could happen, we then have nothing against Communism and its economic program or political program in general."

We feel that a commentary is redundant here. Nikolai's position toward the liberation war is clear and is consistent with his further conduct. In his writings in Dachau toward the end of 1944 (*Words to the Serbian People Through the Prison Window*, written and preserved on small pieces of paper) he clearly welcomed the arrival of freedom: "Here is our state once again! Here is our golden freedom once again! Thanks and glory to You Lord, for Your gift... Help, O Lord, everyone, and the Serbs, too, to repent, to correct themselves and to cleanse themselves from sin, and to glorify You." We have already said that Nikolai and the Patriarch were not led out of Dachau by their own wishes, but because of Neubacher, Nedich and Ljotich, and that a single statement against the liberation war does not exist from them.[50] There are, of course, differences in views concerning the content and kind of life and structures the new and freed homeland should have, but this belongs to their respective political orientation, which is the right of every man. It is therefore also the right of a

[50] The Chetnik and other documents, published in fourteen volumes, in book 4, *Collection of Documents and Information about the NOR*, Belgrade, 1985, clearly indicate that Nikolai and the Patriarch were supposed to be "used" for the salvation of the refugee Chetniks and Ljotichevcis as a "connection" with the Allies; in other words, their spiritual and moral capital was utilized.

Patriarch and of Bishop Nikolai to differ in their political and ideological positions from the "victorious" and from "the only ones who can save."

In fact, it should be emphasized that the Serbian Patriarch Gavrilo and Bishop Nikolai Velimirovich were generally of the same opinion both during the occupation and imprisonment as well as during the course of 1945. The position towards them changed the moment Patriarch Gavrilo decided to return to Yugoslavia and Nikolai remained in emigration. This was most likely influenced by the already-mentioned position of the new regime toward Nikolai (already in those days his picture was displayed at various places with the inscription, i.e., the label: "enemy of the state and of the people"!). ("Nikolai was an opponent that was no match for us," said an honest Communist after the war; however, this will not be discussed any further here).

We consider it necessary to add something more here; the reason for this is the "contribution" of the pre-war and Soviet agent Misha Brashich, cited in the third volume of V. Dedijer's *New Contributions to the Biography of J. B. Tito* (Belgrade: 1984) pp. 493–94. He allegedly "discovered" the existence of "secret links between Drazha Mihailovich,[51] the government in London, the Allies, a number of false collaborators, the Gestapo" and Nikolai during his internment in Ljubostinja that operated in a "secretive manner" through "Metropolitan Dr. Nikolai" (it should quickly be mentioned that the "reporter," Mr. Brashich, even claimed that Nikolai was a metropolitan, although he never was). With regard to Brashich's fantasy of the non-existent "headquarters of Dr. Nikolai'" which, for goodness' sake, "functioned irreproachably" between "Constantinople and London," we can only say that Mr. or Comrade Brashich simply ascribed his own multiple-spying mentality to Nikolai, the same way he imputed to him an "impressive mask of mystical acting," probably according to his own "spitting image." What else can an atheist say about a believer, especially such a believer as Bishop Nikolai! (Nikolai would have most probably responded in this way: "To a blind soul, the Gospel will forever remain a closed book.") However, of greater interest, if it is true, is Brashich's information (from the same source) that he had received "a message from the leadership of the

[51] Drazha Mihailovich (1893–1946): Serbian General and leader in WW II of the Chetnik movement, officially named "Yugoslav Army in the Fatherland" (JVUO), a royalist-nationalist Serbian resistance movement fighting both the German occupation and communism.—TRANS.

Party (the Communist Party of Yugoslavia) in Belgrade to look into the work of the Bishop, Dr. Nikolai, who is at Ljubostinja Monastery, situated near Trstenik, with a note that he should consider it as an exceptionally urgent order." We will conclude here for now.

In this epilogue, we wish to add something about the latest label of Nikolai, namely, that he was an alleged "Mason," most likely because of his being an "Englishman." For this purpose, I will present a short letter of the Bishop himself (this facsimile was published in the *Glas SPC u Zapadnoj Evropi,* no. 101, April 1985, pp. 28–29). Nikolai addressed this letter, dated February 25, 1956, to Sava Obretkovich in Gary, Indiana: "You ask me about Freemasonry. Somebody who lives closer to you could give you exact information about that (...). The Greek and the Russian Church have openly condemned it as an un-Christian organization that undermines Christ's Church. Therefore, be careful, brother Sava, and pray to God that others may be protected in our holy Orthodox Faith. There are many smooth paths that lead to destruction, and the true path to salvation is difficult but it is straight and certain. That is all for now. Therefore, appreciate what happened in church."

Finally, I would like to repeat the well-known popular proverb (among Bishop Nikolai's last notes): "Stones are thrown at native trees" and not at foreign or infertile trees. I conclude the epilogue with one of his notes just prior to his death (which as we know, he passed onto in prayer):

"Life, life, life—the most repeated word in the New Testament—is the high tenor of the New Testament, the main string on the Christian harp (in the Psalter). All other values are worthless in comparison to life; but a life that is accountable, for a sinful and evil life is the greatest stain of God's entire creation."

Hieromonk Athanasius (Yevtich)

News from the Orthodox Monastery and Seminary of St. Tikhon of Zadonsk, South Canaan, PA 18459 FALL/WINTER, 1987

Former Rector Of St. Tikhon's Canonized

The Icon of the newly Glorified Saint Nicholai of Zica

"Oh! What a glorious reward awaits those who overcome. They will sit crowned with wreaths of glory on the Throne of the greatest Victor in heaven and earth". Such was the prayer fulfilled in the Church of Christ. It was written by the then Bishop of Zica and Ochrid many years ago and can be found in the reading for the 17th of April in the Prologue of Ochrid recently translated and published in English.

As we read the prayer we know it was a prophecy now fulfilled, for Bishop Nicholai Velimirovich has been glorified locally by the Monastery of Chelia in Serbia, and soon he will be also glorified by the Church of Serbia. For us at St. Tikhon's he has long been honored as a true Saint of the Church of Christ. One has only to speak to those who knew him at St. Tikhon's Seminary as a Bishop, a Professor of Theology, a man of great faith and prayer. Much has already been written of his last days at St. Tikhon's and no doubt much more is yet to be written, but every word makes it clear that a Saint lived, walked, talked and prayed in our midst. Bishop Nicholai exemplified the best of Orthodoxy. He was put to the most severe test of faith during the time of World War II. He was imprisoned in Dachau, the notorious Nazi Concentration Camp together with the Patriarch Gavrilo. He said very little of this very trying period of life, but he himself summed it up succinctly in these words delivered in a sermon at the Cathedral of St. John the Divine in New York on March 3, 1946:

"When I was a boy, I believed, but now I have no need to believe any more because I know there is a God. My belief has become knowledge through experience. Now I know there is a God...my conscience was at peace. If you ask me now: What is left as a living power after this war in ruined Europe, I can answer...Nothing, but Jesus Christ..."

Metropolitan Leonty who loved this remarkable Bishop, gave him refuge, and invited him to live at St. Tikhon's Monastery and teach at St. Tikhon's Seminary and here he came to spend the last five years of his life in 1951. It was a very fruitful period of his life. He lived with the Brotherhood of the Monastery, and they came to honor and to love the wise old man – their spiritual father, Starets Vladiko Nicholai. The students at St. Tikhon's loved him. He lectured, or rather conversed with them on all things concerning God in a language they understood, and in a totally comprehensible way – with great passion and spirit. He was for them an unforgettable teacher and starets (elder).

On the Falling Asleep of Bishop Nicholai, Metropolitan Leonty wrote a tribute dedicated to the venerable Bishop:

"On the wondrous death of the Blessed Nicholai of Ochrid and Zica, Rector of St. Tikhon's Orthodox Seminary (he died on 18th of March 1956)

He lived with us, the blessed Starets
The Beauty of the Slavs, and of our days
The Laureate of covenanted wisdom,
Teacher of the old and the young.

To all he was beloved, and to all he was a kinsman
He never elevated himself,
nor was he proud.

In counsel, he was like the Saints of old
Without a scepter, he was like a prince.

Not a follower of earthly ways,
He chose rather the "Harvest of God"
And like a prophet and seer of the heart,
He led others to the throne of God.

Henceforth You shall praise God
Now you are a Saint of God,
O Glorious Hierarch Nicholai,
Having approached the Most Holy,
Forget us not in Your Prayers.

Every corner of St. Tikhon's Monastery and Seminary is filled with the abiding memory of its former Rector, now declared a Saint of the Church of Christ. We were privileged to hear him preach in the monastery Church, to teach in the rooms of the Seminary, to pray with us in the Church and in the classroom, and for us in his own tiny room where he fell asleep, of which he himself wrote thus:

"We should however leave that [our time of death] to God's Providence. And when we see our end nearing, we should ask God only to wash away our sins, that we may not be ashamed of our life on earth, or of our eventual shameful end of it, at the terrible Judgment of Christ. We pray to the Lord to enable us in time for a good answer at that Judgment. We say in time, because we shall never return again to this life on earth..."

No, Bishop Nicholai shall never return again to this life on earth. However, in the "Life in Christ" in the Kingdom, as he was with us while he lived in our midst this earthly life, so he lives and prays for us, and we pray to him:

"O Holy Glorious Hierarch Nicholai, Pray to God for us – for we honor and glorify your Holy Memory!"

– **Fr. Vladimir S. Borichevsky**

Vladika Nicholai with Seminarians at St. Tikhon's Seminary.

The Ever–Memorable Bishop Nicholai, Rector of St. Tikhon's Seminary fell asleep in the Lord at the Seminary on March 18, 1956.

PART TWO

Testimonies

St. Justin (Popovich) the New of Chelije
Isidora Sekulich
Slobodan Jovanovich
St. John (Maximovitch) of Shanghai and San Francisco
Milica Zernov
Very Rev. Alexander Schmemann
Vladislav Maevskii

Iconic portraits of Bishop Nikolai (Velimirovich) and Abba Justin (Popovich).
(Holy Resurrection Serbian Orthodox Cathedral Chicago, Illinois)

The Greatest Serb after St. Sava

by St. Justin (Popovich) the New of Chelije

Perhaps, a mosquito must speak of the swooping and soaring of an eagle—the greatest Serbian eagle in the history of the Serbian people and of this holy region (of Valjevo.) If the Lord could transform each of my words into Cherubim, Seraphim, and Angels, I still would not be able to worthily, or even close to worthily, laud the greatest Serb after St. Sava, the Equal-to-the-Apostles, the Holy Bishop Nikolai of Serbia.

The Serbian Church and the Serbian people possess two men. The first, St. Sava, was the only one until now to be called Equal-to-the-Apostles. Forgive us, Holy Master, because, for me and for every healthy Serbian soul, you are the second Equal-to-the-Apostles, Bishop of Zhicha and Holy Serbian Chrysostom!

And everything he spoke was a heavenly treasure. Everything he wrote was incorruptible. Heavenly, eternal gold. Truly, if you were to journey past the great Saints of God, past the great and holy authors of Christ's Church, following St. John Chrysostom, the shining sun of Constantinople, nearest to him would be the Holy Bishop Nikolai, St. Damascene, Gregory Palamas and the rest.

...Every one of his words is a song, an eternal song, a song about Eternity. A song about the Eternal Truth, a song about Eternal Righteousness, a song of the One and True God of all worlds—the Lord Christ ...

Today, we Serbs have him, the Serbian St. Basil the Great, and truly is he Great. And we encounter every mystery, the great mysteries, the mysteries of all God's worlds, in his works. Remember his sermons which he gave as a young hieromonk, and his delightful hymns to the Lord Christ, and his Akathist to Christ the Resurrector. His holy and great soul encompassed every being, from the tiniest to the Archangels. His immense intellect gave the Serbian man and Serbian nation a science which had never been known. Until him, they were all mute, all tongue-tied! Through him spoke the Serbian spirit, through him spoke the brilliance of St. Sava, through him, the deafened Serbian soul spoke thunderously and like a Cherubim. Deafened from politics, from party politics... Deafened to everything eternal, to everything which is Christ's, to everything belonging to St. Sava. And he, a simple hieromonk, a mocked Serbian friar, went through the streets of Belgrade in the humblest of cassocks. They were embarrassed by him and loathed him. But what of him? Over here he created an uprising, the greatest uprising since St. Sava, who is planted in the Serbian race. That spiritual uprising was created by the young hieromonk Nikolai. He began as a young hieromonk, and ended as an Equal-to-the-Apostles, a Saint of Ohrid and Zhicha. This is the philosophy of the Church, the wisdom of the Church! Serbian philosophy, the philosophy of our universities? Alas!

But him? In Serbian philosophy, he is rather the only philosopher. He: St. Gregory the Theologian, the Serbian St. Gregory the Theologian. When I say this, I say this with the greatest admiration, with the greatest thanks which can be expressed. Gregory the Theologian, the greatest intellect, perceiving the mysteries of the Divine Beings more than any other man through the gift of God. Lo, the Lord gave to the Serbian race something similar. The eternal Serbian Gregory the Theologian.

But this mosquito has more to buzz about! An evangelist among the holy Evangelists. Here is a Serbian Holy Evangelist. Every one of his words is the good news. Every word—a tiny Gospel. As with a fragrant root, the more you scratch it, the greater the fragrance. Hence,... the more you read him, the more you pray through his readings and the more you sense the Heavenly, archangelic fragrance in his works. It is like the Eternal Gospel, that Gospel which the Angels seek to glimpse (2 Peter 1:11; Rev. 14:6). He himself spoke this Gospel to us Serbs most eloquently. Most eloquently for man, and even for the Angels.

Among the Holy Apostles, there he is, the Serbian Holy Apostle! Oh, who could have ever traversed the Serbian lands, proclaiming Christ's Gospel and Christ's Good-news as he did? From Ohrid to Budim, from Pirot to Vranje, from Prohor Pcinjski to Rijeka. There is no one like him, the Apostle-Bishop. The Apostle and Bishop—the Equal to the Apostles, the Holy Bishop Nikolai.

Here is the greatest Serbian Martyr after St. Sava;... the Holy Bishop who was a Martyr on this earth. Those who know, who know his most intimate life, know of his frequent weeping. They know of his sobbing at

Ljubostinje during the war. The Germans, our enemies in those times, they knew what Bishop Nikolai meant for them. That his mouth was to be gagged, and he was to be silenced. In silencing him, silencing the entire Serbian race. Lo, he who in holy Ljubostinje wept over the pains and toiling of the Serbian race, became a prisoner in the monastery of Vojlovice, only to be taken to Dachau later to die for the sake of God, and for the sake of all Serbs. A martyr above martyrs—that was Bishop Nikolai!

And today, today he still weeps in Heaven more than he rejoices over us Serbs here on this earth. And for his sake? What is most important for a Saint of God, for a man who from heaven sees all worlds? What is central? God, the True God. His Eternal Righteousness—the Lord Christ. Yet what are the Serbs doing to the Lord Christ? What are the Serbs doing with their faith? What are the Serbs doing with their slava? Cowards! Many do not celebrate, many remove their icons from their homes, many hide them in their closets, they hide them in their basements and attics.[1] A shameless flock, the blind fallen flock of St. Sava. What is this, what sort of rabbit-like spirit has entered the Serbian soul? Where is Obilic? Where is Obilic to defend his faith, to defend his eternal honor, to defend his history? Indeed, a Holy Serbian Martyr, that is what Bishop Nikolai is.

Among the Holy Confessors, here is the Serbian Holy Confessor, equal to St. Maximus the Confessor, St. Theodore the Studite, St. Nicholas the Georgian Confessor and many other Holy Confessors. He was able to, with such ability, such fearlessness, proclaim and confess the Truth of the Lord Christ. Your truth, oh unfortunate Serb! The truth of all of Serbian history! The truth of the entire human race. There is no one like him, nobody who has ever proclaimed (Christ) as such to the Serbian race.

When during difficult hardships many Serbian mouths were shut, he said to the German tyrants, "Here I am before my flock. You fire your weapons upon my children in Kraljevo, so I have come that you may first shoot me and then them." The German officer and commander was bewildered. He (Nikolai) spoke with a fluent German tongue.

Then at Ljubostinja. while Professor Pesic and others were with him, he was taken to Krusevac under the guard of German soldiers. There, he held himself together fearlessly. He told the whole truth to the Germans, he predicted everything. Indeed, he was truly a Serbian Holy Man.

[1] This was written during the Communist period in Yugoslavia.—Ed.

Among the wise men, among the physicians, among the wonderworkers, here is the Holy Serbian Physician—the Holy Bishop Nikolai. Tell me, who can number all the souls that Bishop Nikolai healed with his words and his prayers across the Serbian nation?! Who can number the sick that he cured? Who can number the multitude of people with a troubled conscious whom the Holy Bishop healed, giving them true faith in the True God. Who? Truly, he is a Physician of souls and of the Serbian conscience. The Heavenly Physician of the Serbian conscience.

Yet among the Holy Benefactors— who is he? He is the New Serbian Benefactor. The greatest after St. Nemanja. Indeed, you are the witnesses of this. From Ohrid to Zhicha, he raised and restored monasteries both throughout the heart of Sumadija, and outside of Sumadija. Everywhere is his spirit. Him, the restless builder, the restless *Neimar* (developer and builder), restoring the legacy of St. Nemanja.

Oh earthly Serbia! Where was Bishop Nikolai born? And where did he repose? Abroad! You, Serb, were not worthy that the greatest Serb after St. Sava should expire in Serbia and send his soul into the other world where St. Sava awaits him. There was much distress in the soul of the great St. Sava when he left this world and died in Bulgaria. A lesson for the Serbian rulers of those times, for the Serbian land, for the Serbian people. And yet here is another lesson, another historical lesson being repeated. Bishop Nikolai reposes in America, there in Libertyville.[2] This is symbolic, my dear and dearest brothers. Symbolic and dreadful. The second greatest man dies outside of our lands. Oh, how unworthy we are! Oh, how shameful it is to be the man who has betrayed even his greatest people, his greatest Saints. Oh, how dreadful it is to be a Serb without Christ! How dreadful it is to be a Serb without St. Sava! Without the Holy Bishop Nikolai!...

Today Heavenly Serbia, today, not only Heavenly Serbia, but the Heavenly Orthodox Church, celebrates its greatest witness of the Serbian race after St. Sava—the Holy, Equal-to-the-Apostles, the Serbian Nikolai. Today the Seraphim and Cherubim celebrate him, for he is equal to them according to the Good News which he spread across the earth, to all the lands of Europe, America, and Asia, as a Cherubim! Today he is certainly embraced by whom? It is St. Sava who embraces his most beloved son of the Serbian race. And with him, around him, the multitude of Serbian Saints, with St. Sava, St. Simeon the Myrrh-gusher and the rest of the Ser-

[2] His relics were translated to Serbia in 1989.—Ed.

bian Saints. Today in the heavens, Heavenly Serbia celebrates its greatest Serbian Saint. Today all the Saints, all the nobles, all of the Holy Nemanjices in heaven, greet the new Serbian Martyr, the greatest new Serbian Evangelist, the greatest new Serbian Apostle—the Holy Bishop Nikolai.

Today all those who died "for the Honorable Cross and Golden Freedom," all those who were expelled by the IDC (Independent State of Croatia), every one of the more than hundreds of thousands of Serbs who for the sake of the Orthodox faith lost their lives, they all stand on their feet in prayer and celebrate the greatest Serb, the Holy Bishop Nikolai. And it will be spoken of in Belgrade, it will be spoken of in Skoplje, in Zagreb, in Moscow, in Washington, it will be spoken of throughout the earth! Lelich, it was Lelich that gave the Serbian race is greatest Saint, the greatest man after St. Sava.

We Serbs of today do not know what we have. But lo, God has sent us a Prophet, and an Apostle, and an Evangelist! But why are we, our generation, the worst Serbs? Because we have betrayed all that must not be betrayed! Because we betray the Lord God, His Truth, Eternal Life, the Heavenly Kingdom! Betrayed in exchange all that which you see with your eyes, for cinemas, for theatres and for bodily entertainment!

Alas! Alas! Let us pray to the Holy Bishop Confessor to save us from hell, from our deepest hell. We Serbs of today. May he line us up in his Heavenly army, may he give us the fearlessness of the Cherubim so that we may love and cherish the Lord Christ above all, as he does. That is his will. His entire life is a will and a testament of St. Sava and of Kosovo: Sacrificing all for Christ, and Christ for nothing! That is the will of the Holy Bishop Nikolai. That is will of St. Sava. That is the will of the Holy Tsar Lazar of Kosovo.

There is no greater Teacher, there is no greater Heavenly bell above the Serbian lands than the Holy Bishop Nikolai. A thunderer like St. Elijah, but also kind and merciful following the Lord Christ. We, it is we who have but one path, one escape from our hell, the one and only path to our heaven—that is the path of St. Sava and St. Nikolai.

May the good Lord awaken Serbian souls to all that is eternal, to all that is holy. And may the Holy Bishop Nikolai multiply his prayers in Heavenly Serbia for us who have sinned much on this earth. May he, together with St. Sava and all the Serbian Saints, entreat the Lord Christ that He bring the Serbs to wisdom, bring the Serbs to their senses, bring the Serbs to faith. That He may resurrect them from their countless graves. Graves of selfishness, of brotherly hatred, of fratricide. Alas for every dissension and misfortune. Hatred has bewitched the Serbs. Lord, remove the hatred of one's brother from Serbian souls.

Holy Confessor, together with all the Saints, pray for us, that the Serbs come to their senses. That brothers make peace, that divisions, the greatest plague, are put to an end—the plague of today which has infected the Serbian people.

Holy Confessor and Equal-to-the-Apostles, forgive me—a mosquito of the Serbian land—for having bumbled against either you or myself. Amen.

Archimandrite Justin (Popovich) (1966)[3]
Translated by Dushan Radosavljevic

⁘ ⁘ ⁘

A Reflection on Nikolai's *Prayers by the Lake*

by St. Justin (Popovich) the New of Chelije

Our national soul, encapsulated in a national body, has stammered and suffered for centuries, searching for a language able to speak of its wounds, its sorrows, its yearnings, and its prayers. And it found its own tongue, it found it in *Bishop Nikolai.* In him our stuttering soul has broken itself in sobbing—he whose depth our eyes have yet to perceive, whose eloquent prayers our ears have yet to comprehend. He is a God-sent tongue that stands before our souls, blazingly and dreadfully confessing the Three-sunned Lord of All-Worlds. He has a style: a graceful, marvelous manner of soul. He speaks as no man has ever spoken among us. He prays; no man among us has ever prayed as eloquently as he. He has a gift of words, for he has the gift of awareness, the gift of graciousness, the gift of all-encompassing love, the gift of prayer. Beside him, we were desperate; the yearning for Christ within our souls had been extinguished; it had dried out and faded. From him we quivered with joy; the yearning for Christ within our souls came to

[3] This sermon was delivered at the ten-year memorial of the Holy Bishop Nikolai at his church-endowment in Lelich. Though Fr. Justin had given many more of these sermons at this annual memorial in Lelich, only seven of them were kept and published (*Selected Works of Fr. Justin, book 1: Feastday Sermons* [Belgrade, 1998]). Each one of them newly acclaims and hymns Bishop Nikolai as a *Saint.*—Ed.

life through him, it resurrected and became young. The flame of Rastko's[4] yearning for Christ settled in him and flared into a great blaze; and he burns in that blaze, he burns in a sacrifice of whole burnt offerings for all (Christ's) people. For this reason he became our hope, our hope in the dark days of our despairing modernity. We are present at a great and rare wonder, a marvelous and holy sign of the times; the first time, the blessed Eternity of the Holy Trinity anchored in Rastko, and Rastko's yearning for Christ turned him into the Christ-bearing Sava; for a second time that same Eternity has anchored itself again in Bishop Nikolai, and in our eyes, turning Nikolai's yearning for Christ into the Christ-bearing Nikolai...

From St. Sava, from then until today, our Orthodoxy has not had a more eloquent or able confessor than Bishop Nikolai. With prayerful adoration, our descendents will be sustained and bettered by him, as we by St. Sava. Our descendents will both marvel and mourn at what we have heard with our ears. For them, as for many of us, he will be this: a hearth where those frozen with skepticism and with little faith can thaw themselves out and warm up. But of this we shall, if God permits, speak with greater detail in our study on Bishop Nikolai...[5]

With prayer he thinks, with prayer he philosophizes. One can sense the light-bearing spirits of the great Orthodox ascetics that speak through him, especially the magnificent spirit of St. Simeon the New Theologian. With prayer he feels God, with prayer he feels all of creation. He is in a prayerful relationship with everything. And it is Orthodoxy which leads him, only Orthodoxy. The soul is entirely collected in prayer, and through endless complicated wonders, known as the world, it goes forth led by prayer, for prayer is the only guide of the intellect, heart, and will possessing vision.

He speaks of Christ because he lives in Him. He spreads his mysterious personhood to theanthropic proportions; he experiences personally and experientially the Divine-incarnation and birth of Christ in his own soul. That reminds us of the grace-filled experiential Christology of St. Makari-

[4] Rastko was St. Sava's name before the monastic tonsure.—ED.

[5] Fr. Justin never fulfilled this wish. He told us many times that after completing *The Lives of the Saints*, he would then write *The Life of the Holy Bishop Nikolai*. He never got to it. But this, his *testimony of Nikolai* (which we reference here in this extract) indisputably shows that he considered him to be a *Saint* even while he was still alive. He told us, and repeated on several occasions: "I prayed *for* Bishop Nikolai for only four days after he reposed. I could not bring myself to do so anymore, and since then I began to pray *to* him."

os the Great. The idea is as such: to give birth to Christ in oneself (Gal. 4:19), becoming God, for that is why God became food for men...

Prayer widens the boundaries of man to the All-man (=Christ); it makes man sensitive to every wound and sin: it makes man capable of weeping in his eyes for all those in tears, and of suffering with the suffering of those in sorrow. Through the beautiful prayers of our Psalmist (Nikolai) flows the spirit of the All-man (=Christ). The boundaries of time and space disappear; prayer breathes with a universal spirit: what speaks is not a slave of time and space, not a man, but the All-man. Through his soul's yearning for Christ we are in love with Christ, and while the slaves of time and space slaughter in order to spend the riches of the earth, our fearless warrior (Nikolai) stands for eternity on the dead side of our soul, kneeling, prostrating, sobbing and praying for all (Christ's) people.

O Lord Who loves mankind, imbue me with the prayerfulness of our Father, Bishop Nikolai.[6]

Hieromonk Justin (Popovich) (1923)
Translated by Dushan Radosavljevic

⁘ ⁘ ⁘

Spiritual Heroism

by Isidora Sekulich

Is there anything more delightful than the sight of a man who has a vocation and expends his effort in developing it? I am always drawn back to the region of Zhicha where I find our present great spiritual and historical architect, namely His Grace Nikolai, Bishop of Zhicha. His Grace Nikolai's vocation is clearly visible in his person and works just as the resplendent cupola is clearly visible at his Zhicha; and just as Zhicha's yellow belfry will soon be seen and heard again. The ancient monasteries on both banks of the Morava River in the Ovchar-Kablar Gorge also sparkle like fireflies in the night, as they are being restored and becoming active once again. May all twelve of these monasteries rise again! A vocation is a special assignment from God and, what is more, it involves a conscious decision of an individual in favor of his people. The fulfillment of a vocational task is hard to accomplish; it requires great fervency, at times enor-

[6] *Christian Life*, no. 1–2, yr. II (1923), pp. 75–78.—Ed.

mous exertion, and is a great joy to the struggler who sees the creation of something that is not yet visible to other people.

His Grace Nikolai is easily accessible in Kraljevo; he is uncomplicated and kind. He is always very patient, listens to you attentively, and has something pleasant to tell you, true to his vocation; he befriends your soul. His Grace does not speak about his own works. Indeed, who would be able to understand him were he to begin to speak about all the aspects of his work, the variety of people he works with, the dependence on public means, and how God contributes to man's spiritual growth and always finishes what is worthy of completion.

His Grace sits in a chair in a rather strange manner, making himself shorter in order to gaze in front of him as if he were looking at some seashore. After a while, you too, start to gaze along this same seashore upon which no one is sailing; His Grace Nikolai grows into a seashore boulder. He has the difficult task of swaying just like a water plant and expanding this delicate movement farther and deeper into the sea. His Grace has traveled the world and has seen different peoples and realities; he, too, has been noticed and observed by many people of the world. During this time, in his search of where and how to fit into his vocation, he found Ohrid and Bitolj, and Shumadija, places of monasteries and traditions of prayer. He began his difficult mission here working at the development and growth of a strong movement.

You cannot approach His Grace's work in an academic way, using procedures and analyses. It is not tangible; its essence is connected to the coarse earth and to its people. You cannot detect a method, scientific or artistic, or a five-year strategy. There are no drawn-up plans or stacks of bills in his pockets. His Grace does not possess a cash register full of money. Nikolai is a spiritual architect: he follows his vocation. His co-workers are the many simple and nameless people; they surpass those whose names are renowned, for simple people possess the joy of giving: "The people rejoiced because they gave freely," we read in the Old Testament.

His Grace Nikolai has revived the old foundations of our monasteries, of every style and tradition. They are rising once again the way St. Sava, our previous rulers, and chief priests had intended them, not only as churches and sanctuaries, but also as great national and cultural institutions that shape the entire life of the people and the state. They are the key elements that strengthen the religious ideals in every area of public life, for we are a people for whom the "Kingdom of Heaven" has always been the decisive force in our history and politics.

Does His Grace Nikolai have enough helpers; does he have enough like-minded people for this colossal undertaking, for the awakening of foundations? Certainly, there are many co-workers with similar ideas and national sentiments; we fear, however, that they do not measure up to his visions and aspirations.

This man has seen many a monastery and realizes that Zhicha alone represents the exception. In any case, only Zhicha has its own justification. Indeed Zhicha is an exception among the monasteries. "In actual geographical terms" the monastery stands at strategic crossroads. Its position and history argue the need for its establishment as an institution in the spirit of St. Sava, namely, as the organizational and administrative center of a large territory of monasteries and settlements that, in a certain sense, encompasses the entire Serbian people.

His Grace Nikolai faces much criticism and difficulties of every sort. He perceives them as he gazes at the beautiful pine trees outside his windows that are, "so peaceful even though a hell of conflicts and unrest reigns over the world," as he himself expressed. Most probably he finds serenity in those pine trees as he contemplates the cares, knowledge, and the good will of humble people as well as the ill will of those who are at war with each other and who, according to the prophet Isaiah, "destroy houses in order to fortify a wall."

The monasteries would guide the people through temptations and lead them safely to the next world ... Could a handful of monasteries, such as those of the Ovchar-Kablar Gorge or those situated in southern Serbia, or in Frushka Gora, gather enough spiritual strength from their region to do this? Could a monastery like Zhicha with all its components, from the altar to the printing shop, be a mediator for an alliance between the Church, the state and the people? Could Zhicha be a mediator for that political force that St. Sava found, which consisted of the unity of the people around one value that is from the world above?

It must be possible to establish a strong spiritual life and to erect spiritual edifices upon the monastic foundations. Surely, he is not mistaken who believes that monasticism is a concentration of spirituality in one place and that this concentration represents a vocation, which demands spiritual heroism.

His Grace has been an avid reader and a student his whole life!... An observer is sometimes saddened and at other times confused, but His Grace Nikolai is calm. He knows what we do not know, and he has thoughts that we do not have... His Grace is always calm. He is not a lover of catastrophes and of catastrophic presentiments, as long as there are people who believe in God and who work through the Spirit. He has said countless times in his sermons that one should be afraid of nothing on this earth. One should not fear death itself. Virgil expressed this in a Latin verse: "Is it so hard to die?" But His Grace Nikolai says, "Those that have died, are alive," and His Grace's endurance emanates from that; he is at peace when his work is both successful and unsuccessful. God ultimately balances everything out.

This is why His Grace is so resolute and persistent, as persistent as people are who have a vocation. He will either be the one to welcome or set the foundations for others to welcome the day when the monasteries as national institutions will facilitate the return of male and female virtues to the people again; virtues that even unbelievers and sinful people have valued in our past; the same virtues that ultimately led the way to monasticism and to the erection of the holy memorials. His Grace Nikolai is trying to gird the people with a mystical wall composed of these very monasteries. Beginning with the small Jovanje Monastery, squeezed between the Kablar Mountain and the rolling Morava River, stretching over to Zhicha, through St. Sava's Studenica, and further on in all directions of the Serbian realm, until we find ourselves once again back in Shumadija ... This wall must and will be able to resist all sorts of attacks better than any "impenetrable" wall of fortresses, towers, guardhouses and prisons.

Isidora Sekulich (1940)[7]
Translated by Sister Michaela (Vavich)

⁂

For the Honorable Cross and Golden Freedom

by Slobodan Jovanovich

With the loss of Bishop Nikolai, a great person has disappeared from the arena of Serbian national life. He left a distinctive mark as an author, a Church hierarch, and a patriot. As an author, he ranks among our most prominent writers, and until the end of his lifetime his "style of discourse"—

[7] Isidora Sekulich (1877–1958): Serbian prose writer, novelist, essayist and art critic. Sekulich's lyrical, meditative, introspective, and analytical writings come at the dawn of Serbian prose writing. Her main novel is *The Chronicle of a Small-Town Cemetery*.—Trans.

oral and written—remained unsurpassed. As an orator, he influenced his listeners not only by his style, but also by his extraordinary personal magnetism, something also observed by foreigners, in addition our own native people. In the Serbian Orthodox Church he quickly ascended to the hierarchical ranks; although he was somewhat less concerned with the administrative aspects of the Church, he worked with an even greater zeal and fervency in the spiritual guidance of his flock. His conduct did not display signs of a high-ranking church dignitary; he sooner reminded you of a simple preacher outside the Church hierarchy who spoke through personal inspiration. Only when he felt that the national good was in danger, did he show his strong determination in public life. Then he was ready to stand out in the struggle for the "Honorable Cross and Golden Freedom." On account of his sufferings in the German prison during World War II, he was found worthy to be counted among the monk-martyrs of the First Uprising.[8]

Whoever had the opportunity to become acquainted with him was left with the impression that this was a rare and extraordinary man. Notwithstanding all his literary work and his preaching, he appeared as a spiritual recluse, as though he did not live in this world. He was so immersed in his readings of the Holy Scriptures that events and persons of both the New and Old Testaments were closer to him than events and persons in his daily life. Yet this man, separated from the environment of his homeland, exerted a far greater influence on that same environment than so many others who had aspired with all their strength to become distinguished in public life. The very secluded and inaccessible aspects of his person were a mysterious attraction to people. This was not without reason, for the more mysterious side of his character concealed deeper spiritual forces, which we are not able to fully comprehend, and which are present only in genuinely great people.

Slobodan Jovanovich (1956)[9]
Translated by Sister Michaela (Vavich)

[8] A national revolution of the Serbs against the Ottoman Empire. The First Uprising in 1804, followed by the Second Uprising in 1812, led to the independent Principality of Serbia.—TRANS.

[9] Slobodan Jovanovich (1869–1959): a Serbian historian.—TRANS.

A Universal Teacher of the Orthodox Church

by St. John (Maximovitch) of Shanghai and San Francisco

Toward the end of the past century in the then-tiny Serbia, a young boy was brought to a bishop for a recommendation to the priests' seminary. "What shall we do with him?" the bishop said after looking at him. "Why should we accept this frail child? He will not endure there; he will die and we will have wasted money for nothing." However, after seeing how much the boy thirsted for knowledge, the bishop did decide to send him to the seminary.

This is what usually happens: what appears small in the eyes of people is great before God.

This child was Nikolai, a great saint and a Chrysostom of our day. The little Velimirovich, while growing in body, grew all the more in spirit. He absorbed all the knowledge of the sciences like a sponge that soaks up water. Not one, but many schools had him as their auditor and student. Serbia, Russia, England, Germany, and Switzerland observed him in their lands collecting honey like a bee. He strove to attain the Truth, and not just to acquire much knowledge. Firmly grounded in the Orthodox faith, he also yearned for his intellect to soar to the heights of faith. He did not doubt the truth of the faith but rather sought to sanctify his intellect with the Truth, and to serve the Truth with his mind, heart, and will. Thus, he developed his intellect in order to feed not only himself with its fruits but others as well. The more he grew in intellect, the more he grew in spirit. His human weaknesses gradually faded; a spiritual giant was coming of age, shining through his intellect and through his life. Like St. Gregory the Theologian, "as he searched for the depth of the Spirit, good things were added to him." The little boy whose frailty nearly blocked his way to school became a great teacher of the Orthodox Church, a preacher of the Orthodox faith, a wise shepherd, the spiritual leader of Serbia, a pillar of his homeland, an apostle of Orthodoxy in foreign lands.

Constantly engaged in thought over matters of greater significance, he drew upon wisdom from everywhere—from science, from nature, and from the events of everyday life. However, he enlightened his soul above all with the divine Light, nourishing his soul with the Holy Scriptures and with prayer. He taught by example and word, in every place and at all times, and it made no difference whether he spoke to an individual or to thousands of people who were listening to him. People would gather in large numbers when it became known in advance that the Bishop was going to give a talk; pious and impious people, learned and not so learned, old and young, professors and students. Everyone profited from his words.

With his written works, Bishop Nikolai entered the ranks of the great authors of the Church.

His significance to Orthodoxy in our times can be compared only to that of Metropolitan Anthony.[10] Both are universal Teachers of the Orthodox Church. However, if Metropolitan Anthony is compared to St. Athanasius the Great, then Bishop Nikolai is compared to St. Gregory the Theologian, whose example he also followed. He is the adornment and the glory of the Serbian Church in particular and belongs to the entire Orthodox Church at the same time. According to Proclus,[11] only a second Chrysostom could worthily extol St. John Chrysostom; so too, then, can only one equal to Bishop Nikolai extol Bishop Nikolai.

He finished the course of his earthly life in prayer, and we believe that he now stands before the Heavenly Throne of the Savior of the world, Whom He had faithfully served, and to Whom he is now praying on our behalf.

John, Archbishop of Brussels, Shanghai and Western Europe (1958)[12]
Translated by Sister Michaela (Vavich)

⁂

The Eyes of a Man Who Met God Face to Face

by Milica Zernov

On one occasion shortly after the end of World War II, my American friends invited me for a visit. In the meantime I had found out that Bishop Nikolai was living in Chicago, so I decided to call on him, although this was by no means a simple or inexpensive venture. I telephoned the Serbian Church in order to get his address, and to my great surprise I was informed that the Bishop had just arrived in New York for a three day visit. This was a gift from heaven!

[10] Most probably referring to Metropolitan Anthony Khrapovitsky, who was the Head of the Russian Orthodox Church Abroad from 1921 to 1936.—Trans.

[11] St. Proclus, Patriarch of Constantinople, was a disciple of St. John Chrysostom.—Trans.

[12] Glorified in 1994 by the Russian Orthodox Church.—Trans.

We met. He had aged and had become frail but the gaze of his black eyes was still very penetrating, just as when he used to speak to someone and his eyes penetrated their heart. We began to speak about life in the world, about the Church, Russia... "Your Grace," I asked him, "do the sufferings and the deprivations of the concentration camps kill one spiritually or do they revive people? For example, I have known people, devoted people, who could not muster enough strength to pray. All of their strength had been focused on a piece of bread, on one onion, on a cup of warm water ..."

The Bishop answered: "It was like this in the camp: you sat in a corner and repeated to yourself, I am dust and ashes. Lord, take my soul! Suddenly your soul ascended to the Heavens and you saw God face to face. However, you could not bear it and so you said to Him: I am not ready, I cannot, take me back! Then you sat for hours on end and repeated to yourself: I am dust and ashes. Lord, take my soul! And, once again the Lord took your soul ... In short, if it were possible, I would give the remainder of my life for one hour in Dachau."

The Bishop lifted his head and looked straight into my eyes. I could not endure that look; the eyes of a man who met God face to face were looking at me ...

He told me this, too: "The prison guards approached me, and mockingly asked me, 'Do you believe that Jesus Christ was God?'

"'No,' I answered them.

"They would start to laugh and then question me again", 'That means that you no longer believe?'

"'I do not believe; instead, I know,' was my answer.

"They became irritated and left immediately.

"After some time, they forced a conversation again and asked, 'Was your Jesus the son of a Jewess?'

"'No,' I answered.

"'Well, whose son was He then?

"'The Son of Man,' I said and they did not know what to retort..."

Bishop Nikolai was a pillar of the Serbian Church. Now, after his death, he is constantly beholding God, face to face ...

Milica Zernov (1975)[13]
Translated by Sister Michaela (Vavich)

[13] A Russian war emigrant.—TRANS.

⁘ ⁘ ⁘

The Blessing of Bishop Nikolai

by the Very Rev. Alexander Schmemann

There are only a few events in the life and work of St. Vladimir's Seminary that we can recall with greater joy and gratitude than the help we have received from Bishop Nikolai of blessed repose. We were but a very small and poor institution when Bishop Nikolai arrived and delivered lectures to our students. The memories of Bishop Nikolai's visits on the day of his patron saint are still vivid. We prayed to God together with him and for him. We were conscious of the fact that God had given us the privilege to be together with the most prominent Orthodox Bishop of the twentieth century. He inspired many Serbian students who had come from Europe to enroll at St. Vladimir's Seminary.

A couple of days before his death, the Bishop gave us his blessing and an icon of St. Sava. We safe keep this icon in our chapel. His help and understanding for our work was of great profit to us all. He forever remains a living part of our school.

The living memory of Bishop Nikolai will be the most precious connection we have with every Orthodox Serb on this continent.

Bishop Nikolai was not just a great Serb. He is the manifestation of Orthodox spirituality for all Orthodox people and occupies a position among those who work to eternalize the Orthodox faith in America.

Very Rev. Alexander Schmemann (1976)[14]
Translated by Sister Michaela (Vavich)

⁘ ⁘ ⁘

Bishop Nikolai's *Prologue of Ohrid*

by St. Justin (Popovich) the New of Chelije

In all of Serbian history, there has never been a book with greater wisdom, that is, a Serbian book with greater Divine wisdom than the *Prologue of Ohrid* by Bishop Nikolai. Hence, neither has there been a

[14] Alexander Schmemann (1921–1983): Prominent theologian and author of the Orthodox Church.—Trans.

more important or more everlasting Serbian book. And besides this: there has not been a more profitable book, because this one is of infinite value to the Serbian person, to his life in this world and in the one to come.

The *Prologue of Ohrid* is the Serbian Gospel, the eternal Serbian Gospel. You will find in it everything needful to a Serbian soul in this world and in the next world, everything that lives beyond our earthly death, everything that overcomes and puts to death our sins and passions. Swarm after swarm; a holy swarm of blessed news for you, for your entire life, which begins in this world and continues on through all eternities into the next world. There. That is the *Prologue of Ohrid*, this Serbian Gospel.

Serbian Gospel? Yes, because it teaches you and instructs you in the eternal Truth.

Serbian Gospel? Yes, because it teaches you and instructs you in eternal Justice.

Serbian Gospel? Yes, because it teaches you and instructs you in the eternal Good, the eternal Love, the eternal Wisdom, the eternal Beauty, the eternal Joy.

Serbian Gospel? Yes, because it teaches you and instructs you in eternal Life. Yes, because it teaches you and instructs you how to overcome and vanquish deceit, lies, avarice, lust, malice, evil, envy, hate, ill-temper, fornication, greed, despair, and disbelief, atheism, faintheartedness, and a half-hearted faith in the holy evangelic Mysteries and in the holy evangelic virtues. In a word: every sin, every passion, every evil, every death, every devil, and hence all of the hell of this world and all of the temptations of this world.

The holy writer of this Serbian Gospel is an Evangelist among the Evangelists.

The holy writer of this Serbian Gospel is an Apostle among the Apostles.

The holy writer of this Serbian Gospel is a Martyr among the Martyrs.

The holy writer of this Serbian Gospel is a Confessor among the Confessors.

The holy writer of this Serbian Gospel is a Saint among the Saints.

Bishop Nikolai is indeed an Evangelist, indeed an Apostle, indeed a Martyr, indeed a Confessor, indeed a Saint. He is indeed the most discerning Serbian eye: he sees the invisible; he has the best Serbian ear: he hears the inaudible; he has the most sensitive Serbian conscience: he is zealous like a Cherub for all that is God's. You will not go astray when you are led and guided by him; instead you will always follow the path that without a doubt leads only to Heaven and to the Heavens above the Heavens.

His words are, indeed, spirit and life to us Serbs. They descend directly into your grave, into your death; they lift you up from the grave, and resurrect you from the dead. My conscience? My conscience is a grave if it is not sanctified and transfigured through the heavenly truth of Christ, and eternalized through His eternity. My heart is also a grave; my soul is also a grave; my intellect is also a grave. And when the powerful Christ-filled words of our Serbian Evangelist descend into our graves, all our corpses resurrect unto eternal life through the eternal Truth, the Christ Truth. For only Christ's Truth is eternal. And by living this Truth, we pass from this temporary life into eternal life while still here on earth, and death has no power over us.

Holy Bishop Nikolai? He resurrected the Serbian nation, which from the times of St. Sava until today has never happened. He resurrected the Serbian soul unto eternal life, eternal truth, eternal love, and eternal joy. How? With Christ, with Christ only. For without Christ, all are mere graves and death. The earth is a grave and death; the sun is a grave and death; man is a grave and death; man's intellect is a grave and death; man's conscience is a grave and death; everything of man is a grave and death; his body is a grave and death; his soul is a grave and death. Even the very heavens are nothing but a grave and death; the whole universe is a grave and death; and all the universes are gruesome graves and repulsive deaths. What about you? And I? And we? A row of graves, and a row of slaves; slaves to death. All are mere slaves and deaths; helpless slaves and worm-infested graves ...

The *Prologue of Ohrid* is a most vital handbook, a holy handbook, the most essential reference book, a holy instruction book for every Serbian soul, and for every soul of the entire earthly Serbia that also inhabits the heavenly Serbia. For the same Gospel applies to them from above as to us from below, since the Lord Christ is the *same yesterday, and today, and forever* (Heb. 13:8). Whatever affliction you may have, just open this holy handbook and you will find what you need. There are no difficulties that you may encounter which this holy handbook cannot handle, for it will give you the strength to overcome your difficulty through Christ, our God. There are no passions that can overcome your soul for which the *Prologue of Ohrid* does not have a well-tested and sure antidote. There is not a sin that can overwhelm you or give your soul a fatal blow from which you cannot find deliverance. In the holy *Prologue of Ohrid* you will find deliverance and an escape from sin's most horrifying companions: death and the devil.

If you are proud (and that is a deadly illness) the *Prologue of Ohrid* has a well-tested medicine for you: holy humility.

If you are lazy (and that is a deadly illness) the *Prologue of Ohrid* has a well-tested medicine for you: holy vigils.

If you are avaricious (and that is a deadly illness) the *Prologue of Ohrid* has a well-tested medicine for you: holy poverty for Christ's sake.

If you are irascible (and that is a deadly illness) the *Prologue of Ohrid* has a well-tested medicine for you: holy gentleness, holy meekness.

If you are conceited (and that is a deadly illness) the *Prologue of Ohrid* has a well-tested medicine for you: holy self-reproach.

If you are lascivious (and that is a deadly sin) the *Prologue of Ohrid* has a well-tested medicine for you: holy prayer, holy fasting.

If you are malicious, or spiteful, or envious, or coarse, or short-tempered, or violent, or a bully, a criminal, a murderer, a fornicator, an adulterer, a quarrelsome person, a slanderer (and these are all deadly sins) the *Prologue of Ohrid* has a corresponding medicine for each of these sins, for each of these ailments, proven holy medicines that do not deceive.

In general, if you suffer from any sin or from any passion (and every sin is an illness unto death, and every passion is an illness unto death) the *Prologue of Ohrid* offers you holy medicines for every sin of yours and a holy virtue for every passion. Only one thing is asked of you: to want and to desire a medicine for your sin.

The truth is obvious to every man who examines himself: sin, every sin is essentially an illness of our mind. The same applies to the passions. Sin and passion alike cause the illness of our mind and make it incapable of healthy, accurate thought, discernment, and judgment, and for the accomplishment of all the God-given works of mankind. The mind that has become sinful and passionate, that is, a mind that is sick, leads man into all kinds of mistakes. These deceptions, in fact, are then even employed as truths. This is why man's primary obligation is to heal his mind of all its disorders. This way he can ensure healthy judgment, a healthy understanding of himself and of his world, of his neighbor and fellowmen.

What applies to man's mind applies equally to his heart, to his consciousness, to his will, and to his entire soul. Every sin is an illness and every passion signifies an illness. The healing from both sin and passion is their recovery, and enables man to accomplish God-pleasing, healthy, natural and God-given obligations. A heart cleansed from passions and sin desires God, senses God, beholds God, aspires toward God, and leads man to all that is exalted, immortal, and eternal. The same applies to a conscience which has been healed and which has recovered; it saves one from every deception, it leads from one good to the next, from virtue to virtue. And what about the will? It, too, healed from its sinful infirmity and confusion, desires what is good, honest, true, and heavenly, Divine, and Eternal.

The primary and most horrible illness of mankind is sin. In fact, it is an illness that encompasses all illnesses from which every disorder derives. The healing from this universal illness signifies man's recovery, which makes him an authentic man. And the man who struggles with sin as his most dangerous adversary, and cures himself from sin as from the worst possible illness that has befallen him, experiences himself as a being of dual citizenship: of the heavens and of the earth, that is, he is stretched between two worlds simultaneously, the heavenly world and the earthly world. His being is for the greater part invisible rather than visible. Moreover, a person experiences that man is a god-man being. Everything that is human is in fact human through God and with God. The more man has God within himself, the more authentic he becomes as a man, that is, a true man. And a man completely filled with God is a perfect man, a perfect and complete man. This is the Eternal Man, the Immortal Man, whom all yearn and seek: the ideal man.

All of this is easy to confirm, and easily achieved, by you and by me, and by all of us. How? With the *Prologue of Ohrid*. Let us try it out: let us live accordingly, day by day, night by night; let the *Prologue* lead us and guide us through all our days and nights, and we shall experience within ourselves, and build within ourselves, and finally create within ourselves the Eternal Man. This way we will find our true self, our immortal self, our eternal self, our own god-man. We will realize our eternal self, cure ourselves from the universal human illness—sin—and we will fill ourselves with Christ our God in accordance with the eternal commandment of the Lord's Gospel, "That you may be filled with all the fullness of God; put on the Lord Jesus Christ; for in Him dwells all the fullness of the Godhead" (cf. Eph. 3:19; Rom. 13:14; Col. 2:9).

And the holy writer of the *Prologue of Ohrid*?

He is the all-embracing Serb in the tradition of St. Sava and the All-man of St. Sava: he is the holy Universal Serb and the holy All-man.

Thank you, O Lord—in him we have a new Apostle!
Thank you, O Lord—in him we have a new Evangelist!
Thank you, O Lord—in him we have a new Confessor!
Thank you, O Lord—in him we have a new Martyr!
Thank you, O Lord—in him we have a new Saint!

Guided by him, the first after St. Sava, the all-Serbian Patriarch, we will surely attain to You, O Lord, through the eternal Truth unto Life eternal.

Archimandrite Justin (Popovich) (1962)
Translated by Sister Michaela (Vavich)

⁘ ⁘ ⁘

The Death of Bishop Nikolai

by Vladislav Maevskii

The following excerpts of this text were taken from the journal *Trinity–St. Sava Mission*, no. 2, March–April 1958.

My encounters and life with Bishop Nikolai

I had the good fortune to meet the future great hierarch, His Grace Nikolai Velimirovich, initially in my youth. The first time I arrived in Serbia was to join the Serbian army as a volunteer in the Balkan Wars of 1912–1913. And so, my acquaintance with Bishop Nikolai began forty-five years ago. Following the Balkan Wars, I returned to Russia, but by 1920 I had arrived in Serbia for the second time as an emigrant. I spent the subsequent twenty-four years in Yugoslavia and had frequent encounters, private and official, with His Grace, who by then was already the Bishop of Bitolj, and later of Zhicha. The War and the German occupation caused many afflictions, and both of us ended up in foreign countries: we were stripped of our freedom and were later sent to a concentration camp in Germany. After World War II we met again in the United States. We both worked at a theological academy and shared the same house until the Bishop's death on March 18, 1956.

In 1950 I was in a serious car accident in New York. Bishop Nikolai found out about it in the newspapers and visited me in the hospital. After two months of hospital treatment, I was transferred to a private apartment; he visited me more frequently then. We were both afflicted with the same illness—nostalgia. However, it goes without saying that the Bishop's pain was harder to bear because I had already spent over thirty years in emigration, hence the wound in my soul hurt somewhat less. His Grace, though, was a new emigrant and his fresh wound bled with unbearable pain.

Following my recovery from the serious injuries, I resumed my duty at the Theological Seminary of St. Tikhon in the state of Pennsylvania...

At the beginning of September 1951, we were delighted at the arrival of His Grace, Bishop Nikolai, at our seminary. The Bishop delivered lectures in Dogmatics and Pastoral Theology. From the autumn of 1955, following the death of our rector, Bishop Jonah, His Grace, Bishop Nikolai was unanimously elected as the new rector of our seminary: a duty he performed until his death.

Within the monastery grounds, situated in a picturesque environment above a cliff with a small river, at the end of which a lake and a forest extend into the distance of barely visible mountains, is a two-story white house in which Bishop Nikolai spent his last years. This house does not possess a sophisticated architectural plan or any rich embellishment; neither does it look new. Years have left their trace on this solitary house and although void of an external sparkle it has an interior that still possesses all the American comforts and ease. This is a modest house, yet everyone from even far away knows that this was the summer residence of metropolitans who visited the monastery. The great Orthodox Hierarch, the Serbian Bishop Nikolai also spent his last years here.

So often in life we perceive that God's justice, this flame that entices travelers from a distance with its magical beauty, does not dwell in luxurious palaces but rather in simple shelters, even huts. Sometimes the light of Christ shines in modest houses we often pass by without paying any attention at all. Christ visited the huts of poor and simple people as a heavenly Guest more often than He visited grand palaces of the proud rich and conceited learned men. Let us also enter into this modest little home and see what is in there ... A white veranda is set in front of us, covered by a screen on all three sides. We enter the guest room through the entrance door that leads into the salon and a big kitchen. On the right there are two rooms that can be used as living-quarters. Wooden stairs lead you to the second floor where there are five bedrooms with all the conveniences.

This is where the apartment of His Grace, Bishop Nikolai, was situated.

Throughout those years I also lived in this house, not just under the same roof with Bishop Nikolai, but "next to each other," so to speak. I had the good fortune, therefore, not only to witness his life and work from day to day but also to spend a lot of time with him in unforgettable conversations, when Bishop Nikolai generously shared his vast spiritual experience and discussed many questions about life in complete confidence. Initially, it was only the two of us, Bishop Nikolai and I, who lived in this house. Two years later a professor, a solitary person as well, moved in and settled on the first floor.

Bishop Nikolai and I were close to each other during this time, not only because we had known each other for decades and because we had a good relationship, but also because we lived in seclusion, quite a distance from the seminary and its students' boarding house. During bad weather the Bishop was driven there. The Bishop had a cell attendant whom he liked very much, who used to come from the monastery and was studying at the seminary. This was Hierodeacon Father Kiril Bulashevich who is currently a hieromonk, and is living as an ascetic in Alaska. He is half Serbian and half Russian; his father was a navy officer, his mother a Serb.

We spent the whole time secluded, left to ourselves. The Bishop seldom received visits from Serbian guests. Most of them came from New York and Lakawanna. The Serbs would sometimes organize their humble feasts here, in the House of the Poor, so that their dear Archpastor could participate and they could be closer to him and listen to his wise counsels. It seemed that Bishop Nikolai was very glad to welcome these guests, his faithful followers. Unfortunately, these visits were rare and short, lasting only one to two days. T. Topalovich of New York and Father Miodrag Djurich of Lakawanna visited more frequently.

The House of the Poor is a big building, situated approximately one kilometer from our house, also within the monastery grounds. The house is administered by the priest, Father Sergey Seminin who has a family: his Matushka and his daughters Maria and Kira. A few words must be said about this family, not only because all of its members had traveled from Yugoslavia and had a great respect for Bishop Nikolai, but also because the Elder appreciated and loved them with great tenderness. On occasions, he would go to them even twice a day and sit with them over a "Turkish coffee" for fifteen to twenty minutes. Every member of this priest's family, the children in particular, showed their respect, love, and affection for Abba. It is difficult to enumerate all the acts of kindness with which they tried to gladden Bishop Nikolai. They prepared his favorite Serbian dishes, conveyed his messages, packed parcels that he sent to his homeland, always welcomed him with their hospitality, and took in Serbs who came to visit him; they made the building available for Serbian feasts and helped in organizing their celebrations. Whenever Bishop Nikolai was taken ill by the slightest ailment, the whole family would take care of him.

As mentioned above, Bishop Nikolai delivered lectures on Dogmatics and Pastoral Theology at the seminary. He carried out all his responsibilities with great love. This is the reason why he left a deep mark in the souls of his listeners, the candidates for priesthood, and on their future life's work. All his past students, of whom many are pastors in the new American Russia, remember their Bishop, teacher, and rector with great love.

The listeners were not merely attracted to his lectures because they were compulsory subjects, but because they were something very special, both tangibly and audibly. The lectures of Bishop Nikolai were not characterized by brilliant phrases, sophisticated terminologies, and foreign expressions; the external radiance, which usually catches the attention of the listener for only a short time, was absent; neither did his lectures have any unwieldiness about them because of the extent of his sophisticated erudition. It was his depth and focus, his fiery faith, his exemplary clarity and simplicity in discussions and explanations that pointed to his incredible knowledge and religious experience, which was astonishing. Not without reason was he known as the gifted professor who knew how to influence the youth and how to attract their hearts, not just their attention. Indeed, this is the most important thing.

His lectures were original and interesting, colorful and lively. They completely caught the attention of his listener and held it relentlessly. This prominent and experienced hierarch, theologian, and thinker lectured with such depth, and I would add, inspiration, that other teachers often attended his lectures as well. Everyone desired to hear and learn from the great theologian and this expert of human souls.

He was unusually attentive and conscientious in all of his approaches; in his relationship to his students, Bishop Nikolai was very lenient. He valued only voluntary efforts from his students; artificial methods and any kind of force were foreign to him because they were completely alien to his spirit and to his good nature. His cell was always open to the students; he was always ready to give advice, to provide any necessary information or much needed care. This unbroken cordial relationship, which he enjoyed with his students during his entire time at our seminary was of paramount significance in their education and religious upbringing. The students themselves understood and appreciated this fact very well and showed their high esteem in their relationship with their teacher and, later, rector. One student expressed the nature of their relationship after the Bishop's death, as he said in tears that Bishop Nikolai had been a real father to them, not just a teacher and a rector.

Besides his work as a teacher, Bishop Nikolai devoted much of his time and care to church services and Homiletics at St. Tikhon's Theological Seminary. One can easily say that there was not a Sunday, let alone a holiday, when he served in the monastery church and did not deliver a sermon in Russian or in English. The sermons in English were necessary because the majority of the parishioners of the monastery consisted of farmers who had arrived in America (or had been born here) and who no longer spoke the Russian language.

Bishop Nikolai's sermons were usually on Gospel themes; he taught the faithful about contemporary life and events and offered his wise counsels. Every word of his was full of wisdom and his teaching fell on the fertile soul of his listeners. The senior seminary students took turns in preaching on a regular basis. Bishop Nikolai prepared these young preachers for this task with great care. During their last two years of the seminary, he took upon himself a third subject, Homiletics, as he trained them in preaching. The Bishop would usually introduce the future topic of a sermon in class, then the respective student would present his plan for the intended sermon to the Bishop, and finally he would present it one last time in written form. He would then deliver his sermon in front of the Bishop, his teacher. Only after this was he allowed to deliver the sermon in church. This is how carefully the archpastor prepared his students for the responsible work of preaching.

During the school year, all student choirs of our theological seminary were invited to parishes both near and far. These invitations had missionary goals. Solemn hierarchical church services were conducted and the students assisted and participated in the readings, chanting, and preaching. There were usually two students who delivered the sermons, depending on the makeup of the parish. They spoke in Russian, English, and sometimes Carpatho-Russian. Bishop Nikolai prepared all these students. One must state that he prepared them with great care, patience and love, and his extensive experience never ceased to surprise everyone. Even now, many parish priests remember with joy how the great Hierarch, His

Grace, the Serbian Bishop Nikolai had prepared them for preaching and taught them in their pastoral and teaching vocations. Because of his signature, their diplomas, in particular, have a special value, and are very precious to them, much more than a university degree...

The spiritual figure of Bishop Nikolai

Next to the external world there is another world, the internal world. This world is full of great depths and mysteries, which we cannot find in the external world of activities, no matter how exalted these may be. It is in this world that you will find the kernel of eternal life. The very Heavens are here and yet this world does not take up any space. No matter how much we may become engrossed in it, we cannot encompass it, nor can we be filled up by it.

The essence of our life is found in this inner world. The entire order of our personal life, as well as the life of the people around us, the visible world with all its different phenomena, all are enlightened from within this inner world. This inner world may disclose little external knowledge and only a few facts of external activities. However, despite this tangible paucity, a depth of knowledge about oneself and about everything one is surrounded by is found here.

This is the place where you will find that precious evangelical pearl. A brilliant scientist is blind in comparison to the man who has found such a pearl. The Savior said that His teachings are incomprehensible to the wise of this (external) world. The Apostle testifies that the teaching of the Cross is foolishness and a stumbling block to this external wisdom. It is possible to hear and yet not hear, and to see and yet not see.

To his last breath, this life of the Spirit was the life of Bishop Nikolai in this world. His greatness and power lay in this. His spiritual life marked his entire life and work and gave him such a strength that others could not even fathom. It is from within this inner world of his that he beheld with joy the whole external world with its myriad of simple and complex phenomena. This inner world gave him the ability to survive even in those places wherein others surrender themselves without a fight and perish. He was enlightened in everything by such a light, a light other people tried to obtain in vain by external means.

In situations where people were blind, insensitive, and sad, Bishop Nikolai found a way to be joyful with boundless compassion. When those who were blinded could see nothing, he was able to see through everything with his spiritual eyes. An interesting picture developed: he could perceive one and the same phenomenon in a completely opposite way from other people. They all read from the same book of life but understood it completely differently, as if they had been reading from some obscure scripts.

Let us look into this remarkable inner world of Bishop Nikolai for a short moment and see what is there.

Bishop Nikolai was an exceptionally pious and discerning religious man. His faith in God was not determined by dry formulas and different philosophical tenets. His faith was a living faith in a living God, a God Who is constantly near man, which is difficult to express in human language. He described God as being closer to man than the very air that surrounds him, closer to us than our very own body. He described God as the One Who dwells in our bosom, in the most secret chamber of our souls. In the natural world, Bishop Nikolai saw and contemplated God everywhere, from the smallest speck of dust to the greatest natural phenomena. He expressed this unrelenting feeling of God's closeness to man above all in prayer.

For many people prayer is nothing more than empty sounds, a formal practice of religion. For Bishop Nikolai prayer was a festive hymn in honor of Him Who holds everything in His Almighty, All Wise, and Gentle Right Hand. Prayer is man's living discourse about what is most precious to him, more precious than the whole world and all eternity. This is why Bishop Nikolai was often found praying. He prayed with great ardor in his room and zealously read the church services. He left behind some interesting notes about his struggles and human weaknesses with prayer.

Bishop Nikolai, this rare man of prayer, spoke about many of his struggles as he acquired prayer. As we watched him in the course of many years, we obtained a glimpse of this great struggle he had with himself. Like a watchful guard at a post full of perils that vigilantly watches everything that takes place around him, so too, did this great Hierarch keep his vigilance year after year. When we try to imagine this for ourselves, we are astonished by the immensity of his inner struggle.

Here are some of Bishop Nikolai's personal comments and thoughts on prayer we wish to present: "There was not enough repentance in my prayer." "There was an awakening of repentance in prayer but the measure was insufficient." "I read the Canon of Repentance. I was troubled as I read it." "I was lacking in a good disposition as I read." "I prayed with greater fervor and honesty than last time." These short commentaries shed some light on the secret life of this deeply pious soul. O what power and purity do they testify to! What eludes the attention of most people, and does not even exist for the majority, is detected here in the most minute details and nuances.

Bishop Nikolai prayed everywhere, not only in his room. He prayed when he went for a walk, on his way to church or to the seminary. When the weather was fine, he would take a stroll along the arbors with his lips barely moving, whispering inaudibly, his gaze fixed in his inner self. He would halt and stand still ... lingering with some invisible inner agenda. He used to pray on his walks around the monastery's cemetery.

Frequently and unexpectedly I found him deep in prayer. Those moments are well imprinted in my mind. There he stood behind the dense lilac branches almost completely hidden by them. The sun shone upon the entire ground with its rays. The clean translucent light trembled. Deep silence was everywhere. It was as if nature itself was conducting its own church service. And behold, in the midst of nature's own praise to God was this servant of God, bareheaded and gray-haired, standing and giving thanks to the One Who had created everything in Wisdom and Who is so close to us, Whose breath is known to every branch even to the smallest shrub, the leaf, the blade of grass, and the fragrant flower. The Saint's gaze was turned heavenward and his lips were whispering a prayer. In this intensely prayerful disposition, the gray-haired head of this elderly man steadily inclined further, bowing deeper.

When the Bishop became aware of someone approaching, he quickly regained his usual posture, concealing his prayerful contemplation. I always took precautions to remain unnoticed in order not to disturb the prayerful disposition of the Elder.

It should be mentioned, however, that the Bishop did not limit himself only to ascetic prayer and contemplation. Through his deeds, he always strove to show his faith in the living God, Whose name is Love. In this his stature was unusually great, a stature with which many monastic ascetics withdrawn to monasteries could not compare. He was not a lover of money. Everything he received from his many admirers he gave away to the needy. This is why he died a pauper.

Many more extraordinary things could be said about what took place in the little white house of St. Tikhon's Monastery where Bishop Nikolai spent the last years of his life. However, both time and space do not allow us to offer a more detailed look at the secret recesses of the soul of this great Archpastor who had lived there...

The death of Bishop Nikolai

Bishop Nikolai spent most of his free time in the seminary predominantly with his scholarly and literary work. This part of his work is most visible and represents the richest aspects of his activity during his sojourn, not only at St. Tikhon's Theological Seminary in particular, but in America as well. Those talents characteristic to him, such as his prolific knowledge, his erudition, and his industriousness are best revealed through his works. As one becomes acquainted with his works one is amazed at his extraordinary productivity. The Bishop wrote much, wrote continuously, and wrote about diverse subjects. One can rightly say that as an author his theological work was indispensable to him; something without which he could not feel satisfied. His pen never tired; he was known to write different works at the same time. Bishop Nikolai left a rich literary legacy. Unfortunately, it is scattered everywhere and much effort will be required to collect all his works and to have them translated into different languages.

Bishop Nikolai devoted the remainder of his free time—a lot of time—to prayer in his cell and to reading. And I, who spent the last part of his life with him, whose room was next to his, was repeatedly amazed at the extraordinary fervency of this extraordinary old man, this Saint. God had bestowed such great mercy upon His Archpastor and man of prayer. The Bishop spent hours on end at his desk surrounded by a pile of books, fresh paper, manuscripts, and notes. He contributed to many publications and almost every year a new book of his was published, sometimes more. He wrote in Serbian, in Russian, and in English. He disliked typewriters and avoided dictations. He wrote the old way, by hand, legibly, easily read by everyone. He spent a lot of time in the correction of his works that were ready for publication. He also expended much effort in the correction of other people's manuscripts, sent to him by unemployed "writers."

Much time was also required for his large correspondence, for many people from all over the world turned to him for counsel, blessings, and encouragement. Many from his homeland corresponded with him. In general, Bishop Nikolai devoted his last years mainly to prayer and to the service of his people... More will follow on this subject, but let us now return to the portrayal of the Bishop's life of solitude near the monastery.

It is well known that Bishop Nikolai was not only a genuine but also a courageous patriot. He devoted himself completely to the needs of his homeland and shared in its sufferings. This is why the forced separation from his native country was so painful. At times his nostalgia was enormous and heartbreaking. In those moments it was difficult for him to be alone and he would visit me in my cell, completely broken and on the verge of despair...

Bishop Nikolai approached me also because in our shared solitude, I was partly able to understand him. I was close to his native country by virtue of my family, and I had lived in Serbia for more than twenty-six years, bound with this country in both joy and sorrow. In addition to that, I was also bound to the Serbian Church through my modest activities, and I genuinely loved Her. Many times in earlier years we had spoken to each other openly, simply, from the heart. I comforted him when I could and as far as possible informed those close to him. I wrote and imparted messages for the Bishop whenever he was not able to do so himself for whatever reason.

Once as Bishop Nikolai was weighed down by nostalgia, he expressed how he missed not having a flute, something he loved to play ever since childhood. I immediately wrote to the Bishop of Prizren, His Grace Vladimir (Rajich) and soon after I received a flute from him, which had been beautifully hand-made by one of Nikolai's followers. I remember well when I gave it to Abba; the old man rejoiced like a child, for the flute was from his homeland and reminiscent of it. Often later when the Bishop—always very discreet in his conduct—assumed that everyone in our house was fast asleep, the sounds of the flute would resound with the melodies of beloved Serbian songs. The old Bishop, like Juval of ancient times (cf. 1 Moses 4:21) or like Romanus the Melodist, played his much-loved Serbian melodies and wept. It happened twice that I entered his room and found the old man in tears. We both cried, not only he, but I too, because like him I had lost my homeland, merely earlier; it was difficult for both of us having to face the prospect of leaving our bones in a distant country far away from our homeland...

In any case, the Church authorities who had great resources and means at their disposal left their eminent Hierarch—highly distinguished and prominent within the entire Orthodox Church—without basic care or consideration. Moreover, when the material circumstances of Bishop Nikolai improved, his enemies sought to aggravate even those...

This struggle, however, cost the already tormented Bishop dearly. Morally and physically completely broken, he became bedridden and was under the supervision of an American physician and the monastery's brethren for more than two weeks after this incident. It was then that he told us: "Remember, should I die here, bury me here ... at the monastery's cemetery. Here, I found peace and heart-felt kindness from good people. I pray and work for the good of the Church ... and may my bones be laid to rest here. And over there... maybe someday they will be taken back to my homeland." He often mentioned and repeated this. On one occasion as he took a walk around the monastery's cemetery with the inspector of the seminary who was also elderly, he said, "It would be good for both of us to be put to rest here," and he pointed to a place near the grave of Professor Spektorski whom he valued highly...

In the autumn of 1955, His Grace Jonah, the rector of our theological seminary, passed away and following this, our professorial body addressed the Synod of Bishops with the request of appointing Bishop Nikolai as our new rector. Very soon thereafter the Synod gladly granted our request...

As our new rector, Bishop Nikolai fulfilled his appointment with ease following the death of our former rector, Bishop Jonah on November 26, 1955...

On Sunday, March 18, 1956, all the seminarians and chanters, with the Father Inspector at the head, left for a distant parish on their missionary journey at 7 a.m. Bishop Nikolai was supposed to celebrate the Divine Liturgy at the monastery church. The bells rang at the appropriate time and preparations for the entry of the Bishop into the church were made. However, he did not appear. Then Abbot Basil went to the seminary and knocked on the door of the Bishop's cell but there was no answer. He returned to the monastery church and informed the Superintendent and they decided to wait a bit longer... After some thought and discussion, the Superintendent himself went to the seminary. He knocked on the door but once again there was no answer. He then forced the door open. The following is what he saw: the Bishop was lying on the floor in his nightgown next to the bed with his legs facing the door and his head facing the window. The Superintendent ran up to him and tried to lift the Bishop but he immediately perceived that he was dead. A small wound was visible on the Bishop's head, and his prayer rope, a gift from Russian nuns, was still in his hand.

The Superintendent ran out of the room, called the monks from the monastery and the seminary's secretary. The nearest doctor was summoned who ascertained his death and the time of death, which was several hours earlier...

The body of Bishop Nikolai was placed on his bed and the first memorial service was conducted. Our Metropolis in New York and Bishop Dionysius at Libertyville were informed. The Serbian church parishes in New York, Lakawanna, and elsewhere were also informed. The arrival of Serbian people was expected. The Bishop's body was transferred to the monastery church in the heavy snow and was clothed in the proper vestments.

Vladislav Maevskii
Translated by Sister Michaela (Vavich)

Church of St. Nicholas the Wonderworker
(Bishop Nikolai's endowment in his hometown, Lelich, 1928)

PART THREE

St. Nikolai Velimirovich

A Century of Love

The newly elected Bishop of Zhicha, Nikolai (1919)

A Century of Lessons in Divine and Christian Love

1. According to your wish I am writing this, my daughter, I, the humble Callistratus. As all realities of the universe, with their quality and effects, are only symbols of spiritual reality, so also is worldly love. That which people on earth have called "love" is in reality only a pale symbol of true divine love.

2. All that exists can be divided into the uncreated and the created. God is uncreated; everything else is created. And love is uncreated—uncreated and eternal. For love is not just an attribute of God but the name of God—one of the names of God—and of the essence of Divine Being. That is also how it has been said *God is love* (1 John 4:8).

3. It has also been said that God is the Truth and the Word. Wonderful is this Slavic word *istina*—which perfectly designates Him who is forever true. "I am that I am," in short: I am the same, unchanging... And the Word is the expression of the hidden God. And just as the Truth and the Word are eternally in God and are God, so is Love. And just as the Word speaks for itself: *I am the Alpha and Omega, the Beginning and the End* (Rev. 1:8, 11, 21:6, 22:13), so Love can say of itself: "I am the Alpha and Omega."

4. As love, God manifests Himself to mankind through the revelation of the Holy Trinity in unity. Father and Son and Holy Spirit—one God and through the incarnation of God the Word. In the Old Testament, the Testament of the Law, God is only intimated as the Holy Trinity. So also Love placed itself without calling attention to itself among the many other commandments of the law (cf. Deut 6:5, Ex. 19:18). The world was not ready to receive the doctrine on the Holy Trinity, and consequently, not on Love. But these two are indivisible. The commandment of love, the last among the commandments of the Old Testament, has become the first in the New Testament.

5. In the pagan world, faith in a trinity existed, but not in the Divinity, holy and unique. The people of India have believed, and still believe in the Trimtirti, that is in three supreme gods, one of whom is Shiva, the destroyer of all that the other two, Vishnu and Brahma, create. In Egypt belief is likewise in a triad, but as in a family with bodily love, out of whom Osiris and Isis generate a son Horus, who kills Osiris, which dissolves this monstrous marriage. Before Christ, men were able with their own spirit and effort to create great civilizations on all the continents of the earth, but it was not possible to arrive at a proper concept of God as the Holy Trinity in Unity, and consequently not of God as Love.

6. Islam, though one of the relatively advanced religions, in no way endured the doctrine of God as the Holy Trinity. In the Koran this doctrine is ridiculed. And in the Mosque of Omar in Jerusalem this command is carved on the wall: "True believers, know that Allah does not have a Son." And precisely since according to that religion God has no Son, in the Koran nothing is said of God's love but only of God's justice and mercy. Although Mohammed took his doctrines out of the Old Testament, he did not read the words of the Almighty: *Shall I bring to the birth, and not cause to bring forth? saith the Lord: shall I cause to bring forth, and shut the womb?* (Isa. 66:9). And not Mohammed alone, but also the ancient Arians and the modern Unitarians.

7. Know and remember, my daughter: the mystery of the Holy Trinity is the intimate mystery of divine Being. This inner mystery God could not reveal to the people without law, nor through the law. Neither through man nor through the great prophets. But He did announce, only through the chosen prophets, clearly enough and incontrovertibly, regarding the descent to earth of His Son in the Incarnation, through Whom *the earth shall be full of the knowledge of the Lord, as the waters cover the sea* (Isa. 11:9, Hab. 2:14). And the most important knowledge which the Son revealed would be the glorious knowledge of God as the Holy Trinity, each One of Whose name is Love.

8. The eternal Father loves the Son and the Holy Spirit. The eternal Son loves the Father and the Holy Spirit. The eternal Spirit loves the Father and the Son. All in inconceivable unity, indivisible and without confusion. All incorporeal and spiritual. And as such from everlasting to everlasting, without beginning and without end, without change, without diminution or increase, without influence of time and space, and despite any exterior occurrence.

9. To imagine God without the Son is the same as if one imagined God without love. For all love requires an object for its love. You know, daughter, that when any of the people say, "I love," we immediately and logically ask, "Whom do you love?" Whom, therefore would God the Father have loved in eternity, before creating the world, if He had not had the Son as object of His love? This would mean that He did not know to love, or that Love had not had a part in His essence before the world was created as the object of His Love. But that again would indicate that God, by the creation of the world, would have acquired something that He did not have before, and that thereby He had been changed. That is senseless and illogical and contradictory to the Holy Scripture of God, which has revealed from on high that "in God there is no change."

10. Whoever does not believe in the begetting of God the Son from God the Father, cannot in any manner give to God the name of Father. If they nevertheless call Him thus, they are not speaking the truth. For to whom is He a Father if He does not have a Son? The name Father could perhaps be honorary or titular, as if children somewhere addressed some older man as Father. But if someone says, "God is the Father of all men," do we not immediately answer, "God is the Creator, but not the Father of all people"? He created all mankind, but He did not generate men. If a blacksmith has sons and forged some plows, has he not formed distinctions between his own children and his product? No one may, without lying, name God the Father without recognizing His eternally begotten Son, Who solely has the power to make the transformation from having been begotten to having created. The Apostle of Christ says decisively, *Whoever denieth the Son, the same hath not the Father: but he that acknowledgeth the Son hath the Father also* (1 John 2:23; 4:15–16).

11. In the second paragraph of our Creed we confess our faith "in one God—Lord Jesus Christ, Son of God, Only Begotten, begotten of the Father before all ages ... begotten, not made." Oh, how we ought to be exalted by the Holy Church Fathers, who emphasized and confirmed this truth! Otherwise we would have been liars when we spoke of the Father without speaking of the Son. For if the Father does not have a Son, whose Father He is, why would He also have called Himself Father? And all our speaking of Love would have been only some nostalgic poem without real justification.

12. God as love explains Himself solely through God as the Holy Trinity. In that is the secret key to love, my daughter. Keep this continually in mind. And believe the words of the great Isaac the Syrian: "Love is sweeter than life." But I add: and stronger than death.

13. When we speak of love in the Holy Trinity, we continually think in our intellect that God is spirit and the love existing in Him is all spiritual. The Father loves the Son so strongly, that all is for the Son; and the Son loves the Father so strongly, that all is for the Father; and the Holy Spirit so loves that all is for the Father and the Son. This is the Son bearing witness of God in words: *I am in the Father, and the Father in Me* (John 14:11). Equally, the Son is in the Holy Spirit and the Holy Spirit in the Son. The Scripture witnesses regarding the risen Christ and the disciples: *He breathed on them, and saith unto them, Receive ye the Holy Spirit* (John 20:22). One can only give what is carried within oneself.

14. The characteristic of love, my daughter, is that it desires to identify itself profoundly with the person of the beloved. Such is the ardent love the Father has towards the Son, that He desires to sink and lose Himself in the Son. And conversely, such is the love of the Holy Spirit with respect to the Father and the Son. Yet by an inevitable indispensability, each person remains as is. Therefore also it is said of the Holy Trinity "indivisible—without confusion." It is indivisible, for It is one in essence and of the same loving energy; It is without confusion, since each Person by His particular hypostasis is individual. It is a triple flame of being, of life and of love. From that magnificent divine fire of love we also kindle our small, blessed candles of earthly love, which flicker and smoke, damped by faintness of breath. But what the three Persons carry in full force and undivided, that is the action of love of each Person towards the other two. For each of them longs, out of love, to magnify and glorify the remaining two Persons of the Holy Trinity. That was made clear by the word of the Son of God: *My Father is greater than I* (John 14:28).

15. The love in one person alone is not love but self-love and selfishness. This is precisely why Mohammed also did not mention love in connection with Allah but only righteousness and mercy; love between two persons quickly cools and turns into sadness. This is why, in the Old Testament, barrenness was considered a curse ... Love fully complete is love of three together. On earth this is so in consequence of the way it is in heaven. It is no wonder how the number three plays an enormous part in all products of the Creator, unique and in Trinity.

16. Love has not arisen from earth, but is granted from heaven. St. Cassian said, "Love belongs exclusively to God, and those men who have renewed in themselves the image and the likeness of God." Conscious love refers to the conscious person and not to a principle or an idea or an impersonal creation, but to personhood. Where there is no reciprocity in love, there is no love. But a principle or an idea or a creation, be it of God or of man, cannot love us, though we may love it. Of that love we are not speaking, but of the love that is from person to person and which is "indivisible and without confusion."

17. Only the perfect person, with a perfect conscience, a perfect mind, and perfect power, can have perfect love. Such a person is our God. What every man eagerly desires for his person is therefore that which exists in the person of his Creator. What all people value—love above all—is therefore what the Creator is—Love. And so it has been from time immemorial to today and unto ages of ages.

18. It the inferior is always that is proved by the superior, but not conversely. In this way the human being evidences a higher existence, a higher power, and higher intelligence. A certain European philosopher has said, "I think, therefore I am." And indeed that word of his is proclaimed to the world as something great ... If God does not exist as certainly more intelligent than I, then it is evident that I do not exist, or that I am only some temporary apparition, a ghost fluttering out of the stirred-up dust and formed in an instant, in order only to fall again into the same dust, aimlessly and without leaving a trace. Just the same is love. If love does not exist in God and does not come from God, then it is only some sentimental lust which men have used as a narcotic, in order to be somewhat foolishly alleviated of the great absurdity of life.

19. *God is love; and he that dwelleth in love dwelleth in God, and God in him* (1 John 4:16). Ages and generations of men have waited to hear those enlightening and enlivening words as guiding stars, like the star of Bethlehem. The Apostle said, heard, felt and repeated it as he had received it from his Lord. The God of truth and of love is the everlasting God. He has no contact or union with "agreements" of lies and hate. By this revelation, Christ has overturned all polytheistic pantheons which human fantasy have placed at the feet of egalitarian gods, good and bad.

20. It is not easy to comprehend why God has created the worlds: first the incorporeal angels, then afterwards the physical, material, with man at the top. If the trinitarian God is perfect and sufficient in Himself, in the fullness of life, love, and glory, why has He created the worlds which are inferior to Himself? (We say, inferior to Himself, for no one can create anything equal to himself. Beget, yes: God the Father begot the Son equal to Himself, and man begets children equal to himself in being and essence). The Church—and only the Church—gives the answer: in His bountiful love, which exists in Him, God created all worlds, invisible and visible, through His Son, the Only Begotten, in order to please His Son. Was it for the sake of the Son's pleasure, or for His need? We do not say this. For God, amusement is not needed. His trinitarian love exceeds all joy, amusement, and all delectable celebration. One who is perfect is self-sufficient and has no need for anything, for He contains all in Himself.

21. With boundless love towards the Father, the Son wanted to please the Father by this which was created for Him: more sons for Himself and more brothers, lower than Himself, but bonded in love to Him by adoption. And in the eternal Council, the Father and the Holy Spirit are in accord with the Son for the creation of the worlds through love of the Son. And so it was that all came into being that came into being through the Son. And *all things were made by Him* (John 1:3). And the Son of God is also called the Logos of God, or the Word of God, that is, the Image of God (cf. Col. 1:15–17); yes, God's poem, by which is made known the majesty and glory and wisdom and love of God ...

22. Having taken the initiative in creating, the Son has also taken the responsibility for the created worlds before His eternal Council. In addition to that, He has given voluntary agreement to offer Himself as a sacrifice when and if that should be needed as an innocent and pure lamb, foreordained for sacrifice *before the foundation of the world* (1 Peter 1:20). And so began an incomparable epic poem of poems: an epic of the creation of the world, its temptation, fall, resurrection and renewal. All this as it has been told and foretold. And all with one single and unique motive: love. For God is Love and for Him there is no other motivation besides love, my daughter, you who love God and are beloved by Him.

23. And the Son of God created innumerable heavenly intelligences from archangels to angels, incorporeal spirits close to God. He created them in the image of God, powerful and very beautiful. And He gave them free will. But the sole God did not abuse free will! One of the great angels, Satan—or Lucifer—did use the free will given to him for evil, and he removed himself an endless distance from the presence of God with his legions of adherents and cast himself into Hades, to the outermost darkness.

However, the Word of God, in agreement with the eternal Council, created the man Adam, and the woman Eve out of his body, and placed them in Paradise. But Satan deceived them through the agency of the serpent, and they sinned against God. God did not wish to pardon Satan the sin, for he had sinned in too close a proximity to God. But God did will to pardon Adam, for man was deceived by Satan. God willed to pardon Adam, but not without repentance on his part and appropriate sacrifice. And the Son of God, the Lamb of God, went to His immolation for the sake of Adam's temptation and for those born of him. All out of love. And for justice, you say? Yes, to satisfy justice, but justice is included in love.

24. So *in this was manifested the love of God towards us, because God sent His Only Begotten Son into the world, that we might live through Him ... not that we loved God, but that He loved us, and sent His Son to be a propitiation for our sins* (1 John 4:9–10). Primarily He thereby shows His love for us, so therefore He looks towards our demonstrating our love for Him. Do we or do we not desire—that depends on us—either the eternal reward of faithful love or again the eternal torment of forsaken love. For outside of the temporal—in eternity, time does not exist—all is eternal, be it joy or be it torment.

25. In Jesus Christ the Son, God is revealed as love *which passeth all understanding* (Phil. 4:7). He through Whom the Holy Trinity has created the world reveals Himself as a man of the flesh, so that the love of the Holy Trinity is manifested to mankind, a love thus far unknown to the world. How did it manifest itself? In a manner in which only great love is not shy, as it shows itself for the sake of the salvation of the beloved: by humiliation and kenosis, by service, suffering, and finally by the supreme sacrifice.

26. In the stories and ballads set to rhythm we read how those with love for their intended deliver themselves gladly to suffering for their beloved; sometimes even to death. But the betrothed had been worthy of their love and sacrifice in the manner described by poets. However, the sinless and pure Christ endured humiliation, suffering and a horrible death, not for some innocent, faithful and good virgin, but for sinners and the dissolute, for murderers, liars, thieves, abductors, bandits, perjurers, and the godless, for men with polluted and malodorous souls, who smelled of deadly corruption, and who were dead before death. *For scarcely for a righteous man will one die... but God commendeth His love towards us, in* *that, while we were yet sinners, Christ died for us* (Rom. 5:6–8). Is this not the kind of love that passes all understanding?

27. Love *seeketh not her own* (1 Cor. 13:5), says the Apostle, teaching his disciples by example. The Son of God ascribed all His words and deeds to the Father. *I speak not of Myself: but the Father that dwelleth in Me* (John 14:10) "I speak all that I have heard from Him" (cf. John 14:10). "I have come down from heaven not to do My own will, but the will of the Father who sent Me" (cf. John 5:30). "My food is to do the will of Him who sent Me and finish His work" (cf. John 4:34). *As the Father gave Me commandment, even so I do* (John 14:31). "All that you see that I have is love for the Father" (cf. John 16:15). Look at the Gospel of St. John. Oh, when will the sons of men so love their parents! So, the Son renounces His will and attributes all to the Father. Neither does He seek His own glory, but His Father's. Again, on the other side, too, the Father loves the Son "and all I have shown Him." Nor does the Father judge anyone *but hath committed all judgment unto the Son* (John 5:22). And moreover: "The Father loves the Son and has given all things into His hands" (cf. John 13:3).

28. In love, the Father and the Son and also the Holy Spirit participate in full measure. By the Holy Spirit, the birth of the Son from the Virgin Mary without a man came to pass. The Holy Spirit revealed Himself, being seen as a dove at the baptism of Christ. Full of the Holy Spirit, Jesus returned from the Jordan. By the Holy Spirit, Jesus cast out evil demons from men. The Holy Spirit descended on the apostles at Pentecost. *God was manifest in the flesh, justified in the Spirit* (1 Tim. 3:16). *As many as are led by the Spirit of God, they are the sons of God* (Rom. 8:14). The one unpardonable blasphemy is blasphemy against the Holy Spirit (cf. Matt. 12:31). The spirit of life, power, wisdom, truth, prayer, peace, joy, comfort dwells in those who believe in Christ as in His temple. It continues the work of Christ, uniting the faithful into one dedicated body which is the Church, *the pillar and ground of the truth* (1 Tim. 3:15). And above all, *the love of God is shed abroad in our hearts by the Holy Spirit which is given unto us* (Rom. 5:5).

29. Accordingly, when it is said, "God is love," by this it is said that the entire Holy Trinity is Love. The Father is Love and the Son is Love and the Holy Spirit is Love: the Source and the original Countenance of love between the angels and men, the Source Who is giving of Himself without ceasing and receiving without enrichment.

30. Listen, daughter, to those words of unspoken bravery, which are characteristic only of love. Out of love, the Son of God humiliated Himself, served, taught, healed, fed, strengthened, straightened, gladdened, suffered, was in distress, forgave, and died. *The Son of man came not to be ministered unto, but to minister, and to give His life as a ransom for many* (Matt. 20:28). When serving, He served with rejoicing; when sacrificing Himself, He sacrificed voluntarily, not worrying about Himself, but looking constantly with an everlasting ardent love towards the heavens, at those two other Persons of the Trinity. That is the simple existence of eternal love in the Son. That is the natural way also of men who have love. Because of this, Nilus of Sinai says, "With pain you have acquired divine love: that all will become easy to do and to maintain. But where there is no love, there is no repose." And all becomes difficult and impossible.

31. Love is joy; the price of love is death. Love is sacrifice. Love is life.

32. He who loves earthly wealth, power, and glory, pitilessly hounds other men to serve his senseless "love." And sacrificing for this "love" of his is expected of almost all and everyone except himself. He alone dreads serving others and sacrificing himself for another. Human princes, military commanders, and legions are thrown to their death to acquire for him riches and glory. That is the work of Satan, the man-killer. Not so is God the Lover of man, not so. He lowers Himself from the glory of the heavenly throne to demonstrate, through personal servitude and spotless sacrifice, the love of God for mankind. The love of Christ is the supreme model of courage. That is bravery, before which both death and hell tremble.

33. Let us look now at the beginning of beginnings of human daughters. While Eve had the love of God in herself, she was entirely devoted to God. And she loved God with a divine love, with all the love in her heart, spirit, and mind. The love for her husband, as well as love for all the beauties of Paradise, paled before her love for God. Everything else that she loved, she loved for the sake of God and through God, but anything not seen within the radiance of her well-loved Creator, she deemed not worthy of her love. And all her soul was lightly dressed, transparent, imperceptible to the eye of the body, filled with inexpressible sweetness and delight from the love of God. In her love for the Lord God she could compete with the cherubim. Any desire whatever for someone outside of God did not enter into her heart, nor did she put her mind to it. With love towards God she lived, breathed, and rejoiced. Such was the ancestress, the mother of mankind. Such also was the first ancestor, Adam.

34. Adam and Eve had been gods, little gods, as all the heavenly angels were as well. Do not be frightened of these great words, my daughter, which are frequently repeated in holy Orthodox books. That Adam and Eve had been gods is already contained in the words of the Holy Trinity: *Let us make man in our image* (Gen. 1:26). It is recorded and the Prophet clearly stated, *Ye are gods: and all of you are children of the Most High* (Ps. 81 (82):6). But the words are repeated for you and confirmed by the divine mouth of the Savior of the world: *Ye are gods* (John 10:34). On this basis, the wise Maximus the Confessor counsels: "Let us devote ourselves to the holy Lord, that having received Him into ourselves, sanctified, we may become gods through Him." So also speak many other Orthodox theologians.

35. As long as God is seen in truth and love, shining on the souls of Adam and Eve, they are really gods by any measurement the Creator has set forth for rational beings existing according to His love. That is already reinforced when Christ, in answer to the foolish question of one of the Sadducees, says that men after death *in the resurrection they neither marry, nor are given in marriage, but are as the angels of God in heaven* (Matt. 22:30). The angels then, are called gods by the mouth of the Psalmist: *God stands in the assembly of gods; and in the midst of them will judge gods* (Ps. 81 (82): 1).

36. Whoever was a god, even if small, did he not have freedom of action? Only the great and single eternal God, used His freedom with kindness. Satan, one of the little gods, used his freedom for evil for himself and others. So also the oldest ancestors of mankind. As soon as love was lost, their understanding darkened. With sin, freedom was also lost. If Eve had remained in the love of God, she would have borne children with her husband, "neither from bodily desire nor from lust for men, but from God."

37. In one disastrous moment, then, God-loving Eve yielded to temptation, from the corrupter of her freedom. Satan abused her, the archangel, who had become "the father of lies" (cf. John 8:44), the executioner of men and the opponent of God. He whispered sweet lies into the ears of the woman. In effect, he said this to her, "Eat of this forbidden tree, and your eyes will be opened, and you will be gods. God knows that it was for this reason forbidden you, so that you will not be as He is. He cannot stand competition. He is envious." At these words. Eve's ears buzzed, her spiritual sight was blinded, and confusion overcame her mind. She immediately accepted a slander of God from the conspirator, trusting lies against the Truth, believing the murderer of man as opposed to the Lover of mankind. And in the instant when she confided in the polluted serpent with polluted lies, her soul forfeited harmony, she dismissed the chords of godly music from herself, and love turned cold for the Creator, the God of love.

38. A face does not reflect itself in troubled waters. Neither did Eve see God in the mirror of her troubled soul. She was looking at the tree, full of mixed fruit—good and bad. Looking with her confused soul, she no longer saw God as higher than herself. She had abandoned God. God and the devil did not remain in their true categories. There was then no other woman to support her against Satan and his carnal viewpoint. And with these eyes and this new sight, she saw the forbidden fruit as good to eat, pleasant to look at and giving much knowledge. Oh, knowledge not only of good but also of evil! But the outcome of a mixture of good and evil is evil. In place of love, all is filled with three desires: lust for bodily pleasure, desire for possessions, and desire for knowledge. Having lost God, she began to look for support in things. But the emptiness, caused by draining the abandoned God from the soul, cannot be filled by all the world.

39. Having separated themselves from the love of God, Adam and Eve felt fear—the eternal companion of sin—and they saw themselves as naked. As long as they were steady in their love of God, God radiated from Himself as from His temples. They were externally clothed with light, and barely regarded their own bodies. Now, they were naked prior to sin, but having no consciousness of this, neither were they ashamed. But as soon as the three desires occupied the place of their love, their spiritual vision was eclipsed, and they regarded themselves with carnal eyes and saw their own bodies. Having become poor and bereft, the soul without the blessed love of God saw only what could be seen with bodily eyes...

40. On the tree of knowledge was a mixture of good and bad fruit. And the bad fruit was more attractive, as always, not only in taste, but in appearance, with bright colors and beautiful shapes. Deluded, curious, the woman reached out and ate first the fruit of evil and then the fruit of good. Because of this, she first gave birth to the bad Cain and then the good Abel. And from then on they continued to bear both bad and good, through all the ages and generations of men. Estrangements, conflicts, quarrels, wars filled the whole history of mankind. The history of the world is a macrocosm of the Tree of Knowledge.

41. Some have taken the sin of Eve lightly, my daughter. They say: What is so terrible about a woman having taken some forbidden fruit? They speak in this way in justification, not only of our ancestor, but also of themselves who were enticed to sin. The father of lies has called God a liar, and the woman believed him—is that not terrible? For he said to the woman: you will not die, as God has told you, but you will become gods as He is also, as soon as you eat from the forbidden tree. If he had said: you will become "gods" as I am, that would have been closer to reality. And the woman believed that God had told lies and that the devil spoke the truth. This whole process of separation from the truth of God and adherence to the father of lies, that is of the emptying of the love of God and acquisition of carnal lusts; that whole process, I repeat, originated in the soul of Eve before she grabbed the forbidden fruit. The identical process occurs today among men and women who fall into sin. The soul prepares but the flesh carries it out.

42. When men were stripped of the love of God, the one true love, they began to refer to their lusts and desires in terms of love. Such was the name for the desire for and the enjoyment of carnal delights, for earthly riches, for inquisitive knowledge, as also lust for casual union, for power, and gaining honors, for sport and feasting, for possessing things. Men vest all these with the name of love according to the machinations of Satan, solely and exclusively so that heavenly love is forgotten: the one love that is not counterfeit. It was like a prisoner in darkness, crumbling some black bread into small morsels and giving these morsels the name of the most festive food which they had once eaten when they were free. It was through this lying illusion that it was possible to swallow the bitter bread of darkness.

43. A multiplicity of lusts grown out of carnal love could in no way replace real love nor make men happy. On the contrary, those who exercised them were all unhappy, for from afar they were bewitched by them and from nearby they disappointed them. In bloom it was a rose; after the bloom, it was a thorn bush. Many lusts caused heartbreak, and conflicts, both internal as well as external, between the sons of men. Wonderfully the apostles of God explain this. First James, the brother of the Lord, says: *From whence come wars and fightings among you? come they not hence, even of your lusts that war in your members? Ye lust, and have not: ye kill and desire to have, and cannot obtain.... Ye ask, and receive not, because ye ask amiss, that ye may consume it upon your lusts* (James 4:1–3). About this, Peter says: *Dearly beloved, I beseech you as strangers and pilgrims, abstain from fleshly lusts, which war against the soul* (1 Peter 2:11), and Paul warns: *Walk in the Spirit, and ye shall not fulfill the lust of the flesh* (Gal. 5:16). And still many, many more that are similar.

44. Oh, my daughter, look and see how, with the loss of divine love, man's consciousness of truth was also lost. For love and truth are inseparable. Once alienated, just as many lusts replace love, so many false ideas replace truth, and false gods substitute for the one true God. All human lusts have been represented by some spurious deity. This is clearly seen from mythology, particularly the Hellenic, which has worked it out to the finest detail and, regretfully, with great poetic paeans of praise. Human lusts and passions are projected onto the faces of gods and goddesses, so that men *became vain in their imaginations, and their foolish heart was darkened. Professing themselves to be wise, they became fools* (Rom. 1:21–22).

45. They were the same three principal lusts which provoked the heart of Eve, so that her heart being emptied of love, it tasted the same evil spirits as Christ the Savior encountered in the wilderness near Jericho. These are: desire for earthly satisfaction, desire for worldly possessions that the eye sees, and desire for recognition—all outside and contrary to God and the love of God. But Jesus imperiously drives them away from Himself—not like Eve—with the words: *Get thee hence, Satan* (Matt. 4:10).

46. So said the Son of God in the beginning of His saving ministry to mankind. And at the end Jesus said to His disciples: *Behold, the prince of this world cometh* (i.e., the prince of vain lusts and lies) *and hath nothing in Me* (John 14:30), that is, none of their deadly lusts. He exists between God and Satan, a distance as great as the gulf between vain lust and love.

47. Love is God. It is only through God that those created by God can love ... That is why the First Commandment intones: *Thou shalt love the Lord thy God,* and then the Second: *And thou shalt love thy neighbor as thyself* (Mark 12:30–31; cf. Deut. 6:5). Without love for God all other love is unreal and transitory. As hot weather comes and goes, giving place to frost [unaffected by man] even so, man neither by himself nor with the intellect can love without love for God. Only through God can man love himself as a creature of God. Of self love blessed Diadochos of Photiki says: "Whoever loves himself cannot love God."

48. When Christ commanded: "love your neighbor," He did not think as many do, that it is necessary that we love only the good and the righteous and the healthy and the good looking, but also the bad and the unrighteous and the sick and the leprous, and the hunchbacked and the blind and the crazy and the unattractive and the repulsive and the disgusting …

49. Love is not just one of the sentiments of the heart. Love is the queen of all noble and determinative feelings. St. Theodore of Edessa says: "Love is truly called the mother of virtue, the primary commandment and prophet." Everything else remaining that is noble, positive, compassionate, is tantamount to her ladies in waiting. For this reason the Apostle also wrote to the Colossians that love is perfection: "Love is the bond of perfectness" (cf. Col. 3:14). But to the Thessalonians: *The Lord direct your hearts into the love of God* (2 Thess. 3:5). Truly, love is the shortest way to the kingdom of heaven. Love eliminates the distance between God and man.

50. Listen now, daughter, to this mystery. God is the perfect person; therefore He is perfect love. God is the perfect person, therefore He is also perfect truth. God is the perfect person, therefore He is also perfect life. From this Christ pronounced the words universally quoted: *I am the Way, the Truth and the Life* (John 14:6), understanding "the Way" to be Love. For this reason love is like a Way, set in the primary place. For it is only through love that truth and life are reached. Due to this, once more it is said in the Holy Scriptures: *If any man love not the Lord Jesus Christ, let him be anathema* (1 Cor. 16:22). If there is an anathema, is not he who is without love, then consequently also without truth and life? From this the curse is on oneself.

51. The body can neither love nor hate. Neither can a body fall in love with a body. The capability for love belongs to the soul. When the soul is in love with the body, that is not love but desire, lust. When the soul is in love with the soul, but not through God, that is either admiration or pity. However, when the soul, through God, loves the soul, without consideration for the appearance of the body—beauty or ugliness—that is love. That is true love, my daughter. For in love is life.

52. A scholar attracts by his knowledge, a wealthy man by riches, a handsome man by beauty, an artist by his skill. Each of these attracts a limited number of individuals. Only love attracts all human beings. The attraction of love is unlimited. And educated or uneducated, rich or poor, skilled or unskilled, beautiful or ugly, healthy or sick, and young or old—all want to be loved. Christ spread His love on everyone, and lovingly drew all to Himself. With His great love he encompassed even the dead, long decomposed and forgotten by men.

53. Mankind, even the dead, desire to be loved. And even after death they struggle with death. Therefore much effort is made with testaments and memorials to assure themselves of love even after death. And living and dead, men desire to be loved. Certainly relatives can have the love of their kind, though dying as paupers. But Christ said, *And I, if I be lifted up from the earth, will draw all men unto Me* (John 12:32). Lifted up on the Cross, He has drawn through His life, out of love, all towards Himself, even the souls of the deceased from Hell. Before Christ, my daughter, there did not exist a science of love, nor a religion of love.

54. The beloved Apostle and epistle writer, St. John, wrote: *Love not the world, neither the things that are in the world. If any man love the world, the love of the Father is not in him* (1 John. 2:15). And he gave the reason why one should not love the world, because *all that is in the world, the lust of the flesh, the lust of the eyes, and the pride of life, is not of the Father, but is of the world. And the world passeth away, and the lust thereof: but he that doeth the will of God abidcth for ever* (1 John 2:16–17). These three, then: the lust of the flesh, the lust of the eyes, and the pride of life (particularly for recognition)—are three ancient evils, with which Satan deceived Eve, but not Christ.

55. St. Antony the Great said, "The beginning of sin was lust; the beginning of salvation and the kingdom of heaven was love." Love and lust are opposites. Whoever calls lust by the name of love, sins against love. For love is spiritual, pure and holy, but lust is carnal, impure, and profane. Love is inseparable from truth, and lust is inseparable from delusion and lies. It is natural for real love to grow continuously in strength and ardor without consideration of human age; lust on the other hand, quickly passes, transforming itself into loathing, and frequently leading to despondency.

56. That which among the beasts is not condemned, is to be condemned among men. All our knowledge of animals cannot explicate the interior feeling of animals. We do not know what is inside them, but only what is on the surface. Still we can say for certain that they live according to their nature by the grace and predetermination of the Creator. From their origin they live in the same way, each according to its gender and unerring. It is not possible to speak of sin among animals. But man commits sin if he lives in accordance with bestial lusts. And still such lusts are called by the holy name of love! Neither can man lower himself to the level of an animal without lowering himself even below the animal.

57. If someone says: but man also has to live according to his nature, we ask by whose nature? Is that according to his fundamental, innocent, paradisal nature, as God created man, or according to his other diseased, degraded, demonic, polluted, sinful, disfigured, passionate, benumbed nature? For God did not create men as He created all the rest of nature, but in a special manner. Moreover, He gave them all power over and above the rest of nature. In this man is clearly exceptional to other physical natures: fish, birds, beasts, and raised above all the animal kingdom, even monkeys or apes. Christ came to restore this first and true human nature. And only one who lives according to this restored nature lives truly in accordance with the nature of humankind. Zoology lies under the feet of anthropology.

58. Man restored through Christ lives with a restored nature, and a restored mind, heart, and will. All these three "measures" of the soul are raised in him by the leaven of the Holy Spirit (cf. Matt. 13:33). Ultimately these three components contain within themselves the trinitarian heavenly love, which "passeth understanding" (cf. Phil 4:7). Therefore the Apostle speaks of a "new man" in the likeness of Christ, and in the same way the great Apostle says, *Old things are passed away; behold, things are become new* (2 Cor. 5:17).

59. As the old passes away, and the new comes into being; as rusted iron turns to brilliant steel; as a hill layered with dirt collapses into the abyss, so do these burdens weigh on the shoulders of humanity. For this, a power greater than man is needed for all creatures, even those who despise themselves. On earth, such a force does not exist, neither such love, nor such heroism. This needed to come from heaven. And it has come. For *God so loved the world, that He gave His only begotten Son, that whoever believed in Him should not perish, but have everlasting life* (John 3:16). Therefore the Son of God came down from heaven, *the power of God and the wisdom of God,* to revive by His love the world that was dead.

60. On two occasions, the love of Christ touched the earth: first when He died by suffering on the Cross to redeem mankind from sin and death, and the second time when He rose in radiance and in glory, releasing those who had been imprisoned in Hades. These two seismic events happened and are past. But the upheaval in the heart of man caused by His burning love continues, having started with the troop of His apostles and the myrrh-bearing women, extending through the army of His numerous disciples who followed, and through all the ages and over the surface of all the earth. Inflamed with the fire of the love of Christ, His erstwhile pursuer shouted, *I count all but dung, that I may win Christ* (Phil. 3:8).

61. This same Saul—Paul—writes like lightning and not with a feather: *Who shall separate us from the love of God? Shall tribulation or distress, or persecution, or famine, or nakedness, or peril, or sword? As it is written, For Thy sake we are killed ail the day long; we are accounted as sheep for the slaughter. Nay, in all these things we are more than conquerors through Him that loved us. For I am persuaded that neither death, nor life, nor angels, nor principalities, nor powers, nor things present nor things to come, nor height, nor depth, nor any other creature, shall be able to separate us from the love of God, which is in Christ Jesus our Lord* (Rom. 8:35–39). Know, my daughter, that all the infernal swarm retreats before a man with such love.

62. *I am come to send fire on the earth* (Luke 12:49) said the Lord. That is the heavenly fire of love, from which comes no smoke, nor anything carnal nor material, nor lustful nor unholy. This kind of love elated all the apostles, as also many saints. Their hearts were emptied of carnal and transient lusts, and they lifted themselves up solely to Him, to the one Beloved, not seeking anything worldly and having given up everything of the world for His sake.

63. Such sainted love could be carried only in a person, but not in any principle or law or nature. Even earthly love—such as one can give the name of love—is tied to some person, and not to a principle, or law, or some inarticulate creation. In vain have earthly wisdoms struggled, both before and after Christ, to persuade the people of an impersonal God. It was like water poured into a sieve. Yet even the people who have believed in a personal God, or gods, in no way whatever in their pantheons have they had one God with such and so much love, who revealed Himself to the world in actuality through the person of Jesus Christ, the God-Man.

64. The love which Christ has shown the world, my daughter, was love from *before the foundation of the world* (John 17:24). Such love then is timeless and ageless; it is not exterior, but interior. "I am in My Father, and ye in Me, and I in you" (John 14:20). Where the Son is, there is the Father and the Holy Spirit. He desires for His love to fill the trinitarian existence of the human soul. Although He is the head of the household, nevertheless He knocks as a humble guest at the door of every heart of man. For free will has been given to man, and He does not force Himself on man. Blessed is he who subjugates his freedom to His love. *I will come in to him, and will sup with him, and he with Me* (Rev. 3:20). Happy is he who voluntarily opens his heart to Jesus, Who offers His love, and with this love also life and peace and joy.

65. Out of love for the soul of man the Lord Christ worries also about the body of man as a vehicle for the soul. He nourishes the hungry in the deserts, gives treatment to the people with bodily ills, saves them from storm and weather, cleanses them from evil spirits. He touches the festering eyes of the blind, puts His hand on the leprous and the dead, straightens the crippled and hunchbacked. And the hunchbacked, my daughter, he does not forget. The most repulsive body is not turned away by Him, any more than the most beautiful and attractive. He counts Himself one with souls who develop and mature in their bodily vessels. Everybody with spiritual fruit he counts. And He already knows that frequently the most hunchbacked apple tree gives the sweetest fruit. Remember that, daughter.

66. God knows the value of men's bodies. What is the body? He has said it through His prophets and apostles and priestly poets: a puff of smoke that vanishes, an herb that withers, a flower that wilts, dust from dust. Men look at the cart from shortsightedness and vanity; they look at the vehicle but not at the coachman. He, however, first looks at the coachman hidden in the vehicle. All His concern and love are directed towards the invisible coachman, that is, for the soul within the body. But when He has repaired and cleaned the wagon, He has done it for the coachman. If He heals and builds up the human body, it is because of the immortal human soul. *For what is man profited, if he shall gain the whole world, and lose his own soul?* (Matt 16:20).

67. The Lord Jesus has repeated again and again the reminder to men, that they should not worry about food and drink and clothing. Those are the main cares of the pagans, but not of His followers. It is not worthy of the sons of God; that those concerns which are uppermost in animals should also be the main concerns of men. The one who has called us as His guests in this world knows our needs and attends to them for us. Or do we think that God is a poorer householder than a human householder? God forbid. Despite all our worries for the body, we cannot be saved from old age, sickness, death, and decay. Nevertheless, we know that the Almighty has clothed our souls in this mysteriously woven tapestry, this body, fashioned from earthly materials. We consider it precious, but Him we deem secondary, Who will clothe us after death in an incomparably beautiful body, immortal and incorruptible, which will neither suffer nor age. That is promised to us by the One Who created us out of pure love, and Who reserves His love as response to our love.

68. Love for God expels all fear from the soul except fear of sin. Yes, love reinforces fear of sin: fear of sin that is also fear of God. The great lovers of Christ were not afraid either of men or beasts or poverty or death. They even rejoiced in suffering for Him, Who had suffered for them, seeking only to become like Him. They desired to die and leave this world without delay, so as to be with their beloved Lord as soon as possible. The Apostle testified to this: *We are confident ... and willing rather to be absent from the body, and to be present with the Lord* (2 Cor. 5:8). *For we know that if our earthly house of this tabernacle were dissolved, we have ... an house ... eternal in the heavens* (2 Cor. 5:1). Then he says: *For this we groan, earnestly desiring to be clothed upon with our house which is in heaven* (2 Cor. 5:2).

69. Christ recommends to those who follow Him, not some earthly model of love, but divine love: *If ye keep My commandments, ye shall abide in My love; even as I have kept My Father's commandments, and abide in His love* (John 15:10). And all His commandments are contained in one: "Love." All His other commandments, such as: the command to prayer, almsgiving, humility, purity, forbearance, self-sacrifice, bravery, freeness from cares, forgiveness, vigilance, and joy are simply rays emanating from His love. He who obtains the queen of virtues also obtains her royal retinue.

70. In all the books of the New Testament love is placed above all other virtues and commandments, since it encompasses all. Recognized everywhere are the words of the Apostle Paul about love: *Though I speak with the tongues of men and of angels, and have not love, I am become as sounding brass, or a tinkling cymbal. And though I have the gift of prophecy, and understand all mysteries, and all knowledge, and though I have all faith, so that I could remove mountains, and have not love, I am nothing. And though I bestow all my goods to feed the poor, and though I give my body to be burned, and have not love, it profiteth me nothing. Love suffereth long, and is kind; love envieth not; love vaunteth not itself, is not puffed up, doth not behave itself unseemly, seeketh not her own, is not easily provoked, thinketh no evil; rejoiceth not in iniquity, but rejoiceth in the truth; beareth all things, believeth all things, hopeth all things, endureth all things; love nev-*

er faileth: but whether there be prophecies, they shall fail; whether there be tongues, they shall cease; whether there be knowledge, it shall vanish away. For we know in part, and we prophesy in part. But when that which is perfect is come, then that which is in part shall be done away. When I was a child, I spake as a child, I understood as a child, I thought as a child: but when I became a man, I put away childish things. For now we see through a glass darkly; but then face to face: now I know in part; but then shall I know even as also I am known. And now abideth faith, hope, love, these three; but the greatest of these is love (1 Cor. 13: 1–13). Never was uttered anything so beautiful in hymn or by the tongue of men.

71. When divine love came to the heart of man, with it came everything—all—my daughter: wisdom and power and purity and compassion and righteousness and bravery and endurance and clairvoyance and tranquillity and joy and every goodness. But that is completely logical. For God *that spared not His own Son, but delivered Him up for us all, how shall He not with Him also freely give us all things?* (Rom. 8:32). The entire history of the Church confirms this. By the illuminations of the love of Christ, bumpkins have developed wisdom, cowards become martyrs, rakes: saints, misers: benefactors, kings and rich men: slaves of Christ, wolves: lambs, and lambs: lions. The wondrous strength of Christ's love has not ceased with His departure, but has continued to multiply, very much increased.

72. Christ has given all His love to men. This is why He expects all their love on the part of men. And from you too, my dear soul. Not only did He proscribe the division of our heart between God and mammon, but He demanded something that appeared completely against man's nature. *He that loveth father or mother more than Me is not worthy of Me: and he that loveth son or daughter more than Me is not worthy of Me* (Matt. 10:37), then in reinforcement: *If any man ... hate not his father, and mother, and wife, and children, and brethren, and sisters, yea, and his own life also, he cannot be My disciple* (Luke 14:26). Naturally, that is impossible for all men except those who open their hearts to God. Then the Almighty makes the impossible possible. "Love naturally has nothing except God, for God is love," wrote St. Nilus of Sinai.

73. As long as man does not feel hatred for his old robe, he does not wish for a new one. How could the words "a new creature in Christ," "new man," "sons of light," have come into being if we had not felt hatred for our old sinful soul, which through enslavement to the body had developed a carnal rather than a spiritual existence. An old man is entirely in fear of God. Fear is for us the beginning and the end. In the new man, fear is the beginning, love is the end. Death for the love of Christ is a guarantee of life eternal.

74. Whoever estranges himself from the love of Christ falls into the foolishness of bodily lusts which do not know moderation and are numberless. In those who are illuminated by love, carnal lusts do not rule; they are indifferent toward the delusions of this temporal world. They *use this world, as not abusing it: for the fashion of this world passeth away* (1 Cor. 7:31). They see the things invisible and not those that are visible. Their attention is continually directed to the tomb, towards Him Whom they love and Who has prepared for them what *eye hath not seen, nor ear heard, neither have entered into the heart of man* (1 Cor. 2:9). That is the final goal of our journey and of our efforts. Our shorter perspectives are illusory.

75. Man cannot have true and constant love towards God without first acquiring love for Christ. Neither can he have love for his neighbor without first having love for Christ. This we repeat and will repeat. As it has been said: "In the light we become light." Therefore it can be said: through love of You we also love. For only through love of God, incarnated in Christ, can we truly love both God and ourselves and our neighbor, and even our enemies. Because Christ died also for our enemies. Exclusively through this great price, by which Christ redeemed our enemies, to love them has been made possible for us, and to bless and pray for them. All this is through Christ, and not through our enemies. St. Maximus the Confessor writes: "Whoever loves God will inevitably love his neighbor." We add: Whoever is unable to love God, does not love Christ the incarnate Son of God. In the New Testament two basic dogmas are revealed to the world: the Holy Trinity and the Incarnate Son of God. Love rests on those two dogmas.

76. God has blessed marriage: first in Paradise, afterwards also in Cana. In marriage, two bodies become one flesh; two souls "inseparable and without confusion," two temples of the Holy Spirit under one roof. Why does God unite two bodies in one? Because, "it is easier for a pair on the road than one." For in marriage, impure lusts of the body are bridled: the irrational by purpose. For it enables multiplication of the human species and multiplies those who preserve the sacrifice of Christ. Moreover, bodily nuptials of man and wife, linked in love, and blessed by the Church, are the most expressive symbol of Christ's spiritual union with the Church and with each Christian spirit. And among the first followers of the Lord, the apostles and the myrrh-bearers, were also both the married and the unmarried.

77. Monasticism is in concept supernatural, angelic. In innumerable examples, monastics have proved themselves and demonstrated themselves in practice to be supernatural and angelic. But according to the words of our Lord Himself: *All men cannot receive this saying, save they to whom it is given* (Matt. 19:11). It is given to those in whom the vision of the heavenly kingdom has clearly been opened; whose hearts have been opened exclusively to the love of Christ; those who have lifted themselves gladly up steep spiritual cliffs to the altitude of heaven, and who have felt the call of grace and the power of God ... In this way Christ encourages the monastic life: *He that is able to receive it, let him receive it* (Matt. 19:12). Blessed are you, my daughter, for you yourself have been able to receive that which all cannot receive, for you have chosen the love that is not divided.

78. The Apostle Paul, an unmarried apostle, and with the mind of a celibate, highlights such service in the name of the Lord, saying (but not commanding): *I would that all men were even as myself* (1 Cor. 7:7). And he repeated: *To the unmarried and widows: it is good for them if they abide even as I* (1 Cor. 7:8). And in many ways the Apostle commends celibacy for the sake of the Lord, as much as he condemns the celibate for carnal desires. In the first case love for the Lord replaces all carnal lust, in the second, desires and lusts drive out love and exchange places with it.

79. Monasticism is not created, but is an exception, yet an exception without which the Church of Christ would not have been nor will be in existence. It resembles those irregular verbs (like the verb "to be"), without which speech is incomplete.

80. The great austerity of monastic life in the Orthodox Church is possible only for those who endure, those who have great love for the Lord. Because of it, they have become "the light of the world" and "earthly angels and heavenly men," a model of prayer and fasting, right faith and purity. "Whoever loves to converse with Christ loves solitude," according to the great St. Isaac the Syrian. A conversation of love with love in solitude.

81. In the Lives of the Saints we find extraordinary examples, where a married couple, by mutual agreement, continued to live a chaste life as brother and sister (Galaction and Epistima, Alexis the Man of God, etc.), according to the preaching of the Apostle Paul: *That ... they that have wives be as though they had none* (1 Cor. 7:29). The conquerors of carnal lust were victorious over the serpent which overcame Eve in Paradise.

82. The New Testament speaks sufficiently and clearly of married life. The holy Apostle, with fatherly love and severity, has counselled husbands and wives and children as well. The mastery of the husband over the wife is compared with Christ's role as the Head of the Church (1 Pet. 3:1–8). The love of the husband for the wife is expected to be similar to the love of Christ towards the Church (1 Tim. 2:9–15; 5:1–15), for which He gave Himself as a sacrifice (1 Cor. 7:1–16). The married wife is saved in the birth of children, if she continues in the faith and with love, holiness, and honor (cf. 1 Cor. 7:14). But she who lives in fleshly pleasures, is dead while she lives. Children should respect and obey their parents. There is no kinship without obligation.

83. A consecrated marriage symbolizes the unity of Christ with His holy Church, and in Christ a spiritual union with the spirit of all the faithful. Conversely, infidelity and debauchery symbolize satanism, betrayal of the love of God, severance of one's union with God. But that is in effect exactly the thing Satan desires: to frustrate and make a travesty of the love of God in men. Pure heavenly love is odious to Satan, but he relishes carnal lust and all impurity: *the unfruitful works of darkness* (Eph. 5:11). Those are his lures with which he lures men to the inferno.

84. In the Holy Scripture of God adultery and debauchery are frequently called apostasy from the one God, and the worship of idols. The prophets and apostles have thunderously condemned both those shameful sins as leprosy of the soul. Whether a man has been unfaithful to his wife, or whether he has worshipped idols, in both events he apostasizes from God and satisfies the desire of Satan. Love has nothing in common with adultery or debauchery, which only simulate love.

85. There is yet another offense against love that is as grave as debauchery and adultery—even more grave. That is to be a contestant of God as a hypocritical leader of the people: one who declares his love for the people with the tongue, but in his soul scorns the people. Under cover of the law he cheats and oppresses the people, while abandoning "truth, mercy and faith." For these hypocrites, God is an impediment and Christ an annoyance, and with their guile they devise ways to estrange and crucify Christ. These are the greatest enemies of the people, who persecute and kill the true friends of the people. One of them Christ placed below a harlot and a publican, saying to the Pharisee, *Verily I say unto you, that the publicans and the harlots go into the kingdom before you* (Matt. 21:31).

86. The fragrance of love! When we burn incense, we think of the fragrant heavenly aroma of love. The Holy Spirit, like a heavenly fire, brings the warmth of love into the human heart and, like a fresh wind, chases away the stench of sin and spreads the aroma of Christ to the world. All the saints have borne that savor within themselves. People have sensed it in living saints and in their relics. The Apostle speaks of this: *We are unto God a sweet savor of Christ,* the sweet perfume of recognition of the truth and the sweetness of love (cf. 2 Cor. 2:14–16).

87. The hymns of the Church chant of the "fragrant Paradise." That aroma, emanating from the Lord, flows through the Lord and all His followers to all in whom the stench of human lust has been replaced by the blessed perfume of the love of God. But the aroma of Christ did not affect all in the same way, for *to one we are the savor of death unto death; and to the other the savor of life unto life* (2 Cor. 2:16). For some dissipate the aroma of Christ with the stench of sin, while others preserve it to the end, guarding their hearts and laboring with love, that in all things they should be pleasing to Christ, and receive within themselves "the fragrance of Paradise."

88. *I have espoused you to one husband, that I may present you as a chaste virgin to Christ* (2 Cor. 11:2), wrote Paul to the Corinthians, who were sunk in carnal lusts and infamy. That is the mission of the Church: namely to purify the faithful from all corruption, sins, and passions, and to render their souls pure and holy like the virgins, the brides of the most chaste and holy Christ the King. St. Theognostus writes: "There is no other ascesis as great as that of chastity and virginity. Those who honorably maintain the state of chastity provoke the admiration of angels and obtain the wreath of the martyr." The popular Serbian folk epic chants of "the savor of the virginal soul." That is the savor of purity and holiness, my daughter.

89. In the East the people are aware of distinctions between the aroma of a baptized and an unbaptized soul. Bees, by odor, sense men as enemies and immediately attack. Wild beasts approaching holy men and women ingratiate themselves to them. The savor of love is sensed. Mark how the apostles sensed that unearthly odor of love (cf. Phil. 4:18). God cannot abide incense oblations from strange, lawless people and from vain hypocrites (cf. Isa. 1:13)...

90. Love forgives much. And through love everything is pardoned. Proud justification of oneself is contrary to love. The Pharisee Simon wanted to mock Jesus for allowing a woman who was an obvious sinner to wash His feet with her repentant tears and to wipe them with her hair (recognizing that she had sins as many as hairs on her head). Jesus reprimanded the Pharisee, saying: *Her sins, which are many, are forgiven, for she loved much* (Luke 7:47). For whom was the love? For Him, who was on the road to Golgotha and because her sins and those of the whole world were to be wiped away not by tears but by His blood.

91. Christ, out of love, sought us—but not ours. But men, because of their meager love, seek His good things rather than Him. They expect from Him bread, rain, fertility, health, and earthly goods in general. And He gives all with sadness that it is not Him, Himself they seek. They have forgotten that when they have received Him, they have received all along with Him. The Apostle said: *I do count them all as dung, that I may win Christ* (Phil 3:8). Elsewhere he writes to the faithful: *I seek not yours but you* (2 Cor. 12:14).

92. Love and a dowry are not compatible. You have bitter experience of this personally, my daughter. Where there is a demand for a dowry, there is an absence of love. In the *Troparion* of the holy virginal martyrs of the Orthodox hymnology their love for Christ is wonderfully described: "O Jesus, Your lamb [*Name*] cries out to You with great love: 'O my Bridegroom, I long for You in great pain ... I die for You in order to live in You. Accept me as an immaculate victim, since I am immolated for Your love.'" That is what Christ expects of His brides: their soul flaming with love, and not their dowry. Your three fiancés, my daughter, had no intention of giving themselves to you, but only to sell themselves.

93. Christ as bridegroom and His mystical marriage with individual souls and with the Church universal has been the subject of much Orthodox theology. In the parable of the nuptials of the Royal Son, it is obvious that Christ is presenting Himself as the Royal Son and Bridegroom. But His reference to nuptials rather than marriage indicates that He expects a union in marriage with many human souls, who in this life love Him as He loves them. Not all who are invited respond to the call, for there are many bound to carnal lusts and wedded to the world. But even without them, *the wedding was furnished with guests* (Matt. 22:10). In this way, too, the heavenly kingdom, the nuptial chamber of Christ, would fill itself with the souls of the faithful and with those who would love Him. But whoever was missing, was absent not because he had not received a call, but because, according to his will, he did not desire to be invited by the call.

94. But whatever is likely to be our human destiny on earth, whatever kinds of intrigues and obstacles come from Satan and from pagans, and however many there will yet be in the last times that apostatize from the truth and the love of Christ, still the kingdom of Christ will undoubtedly be filled. Or would He, Who has taught us that when we want to build walls to a tower we must first calculate whether we can finish, would He in advance not have calculated how the kingdom is to be filled? The Church is His Body. What kind of Body would it be without all its members, even to the tiniest cell? Therefore the Lord will purge and revive many repentant sinners—male and female—so that they may worthily call themselves His brides. But only with repentance is a beginning made in the personal struggle for the realization of divine blessings.

95. Just as parents rejoice when someone loves or honors their children, so also the Lord is glad when men love and glorify His saints. For it is the same as glorifying God. *He that receiveth you receiveth Me* (Matt. 10:40), He said. And whoever glorifies the saints of Christ, Christ glorifies. The saints celebrated their Lord on earth with divine love, and in the face of all temptation kept His commandments. So they overcame the ancient monster of malevolence and malice, the first man-killer. And not seeking anything for themselves on earth, they receive everything in heaven. Thus has also been promised (not by the lying lips of man, but by the veritable mouth of God): *He that overcometh shall inherit all things; and I will be his God, and he shall be My son* (Rev. 21:7).

96. Who will overcome? Those who know that they are part of the body of Christ, and those who hold their body and soul to be sacred, not as if it were their own but as belonging to Christ: they will be victors. Those who look at Christ crucified on the Cross and then say to themselves: there is the One who loves me more than my mother; His sufferings are for my sins, and His blood for my purification and salvation: they will overcome. All those will be victors who through time have adorned their soul with trembling love for Christ, the eternal Bridegroom. Yes, all those who respond to the call to the heavenly supper with the Lamb of God. *Blessed are they which are called unto the marriage supper of the Lamb* (Rev. 19:9). Called and responded. Fear of the

Lord is the beginning of wisdom; love is the fullness and the culmination of wisdom.

97. All men are called and God desires that all respond. And indeed many, very many have responded in the course of past ages and still many will respond. That will be such a great gathering as if the sands had come to human life. That assembly the Mystagogue John the Divine described thus: *After this I beheld, and, lo, a great multitude, which no man could number, of all nations, and kindreds, and people, and tongues, stood before the throne, and before the Lamb, clothed with white robes, and palms in their hands* (Rev. 7:9). Such a celebration, such joy, is neither known nor accessible on earth. That is a celebration of love, which truly exceeds all understanding and every imagination. That is the immeasurable, immense kingdom of Christ.

98. Watch, my daughter, and do not deceive yourself. How tender is the love of the Lamb for those who with fear and love answer the call of the Father to the marriage of the Son. And how terrible the anger of the Lamb against those who have received the call but have not responded, if they should reject it or tear it up or call apostles, missionaries, or priests to suffer martyrdom. For when the Lamb of God overcomes all the monsters in human or non-human form, and reveals himself to the world, then those will scream in terror *to the mountains and the rocks, Fall on us, and hide us from the face of Him that sitteth on the throne and from the wrath of the Lamb* (Rev. 6:16). But just and dreadful will be the retribution for love betrayed.

99. When one of the spouses is unfaithful to the spousal fidelity, how much anger, how much hatred, how much noise! In the meantime, neither of the spouses has sacrificed beforehand for their marital partner, not one eye, not one hand, not one finger. Nevertheless, so much passion! But Christ gave all of His Body for us as a sacrifice, all His Blood to pour out for all the souls of men ...

100. Love does not need the law. Love is a law above laws. It is the New Law, or the New Testament of Christ. *We know that all things work together for good for them that love God* (Rom. 8:28). The road of love can be full of obstacles and difficulties, but according to the word of God and the experience of men, that road leads unerringly in the direction of the greatest good.

101. I have written much to you, daughter of God, and all of it can be briefly summed up like this: If you love the Lord Jesus Christ, you have already fulfilled both of the great commandments of love. For He is God, and He is your neighbor. Yes, our closest neighbor. The two commandments of love personally relate to Him, and to Him above all. In older times, men were unable to love an invisible God. Jesus Christ is both God manifest and authenticated Man. The God-man, Who as God showed Himself as the God of love, as Man immolated Himself for us as the Man of Love. Truly I say to you, for that kind of God and that kind of neighbor, to love is absolutely easy, and through Him to love all that are His.

102. O my soul, Cassiana, hasten to foresake all, and let all abandon you. Friends will forget you. Wealth will be without profit for you; beauty will fade, vigor will vanish, the body will decompose, and the soul will otherwise find itself in gloom. Who will stretch out hands to you in the darkness and isolation? One: Christ, the Lover of Mankind, provided that you have been united with Him during your life. He will lead you out of the darkness to the light, and from isolation to the Heavenly Assembly. Think of this instruction day and night and direct your soul in accordance with it. Let Christ the Lord, the King of Love, come to your aid. Amen.

Note: This writing I consecrate to my spiritual daughter, the nun Cassiana, for perusal and meditation and to Him Who is the greatest in heaven and on earth.

The humble servant of God,
+ Callistratus

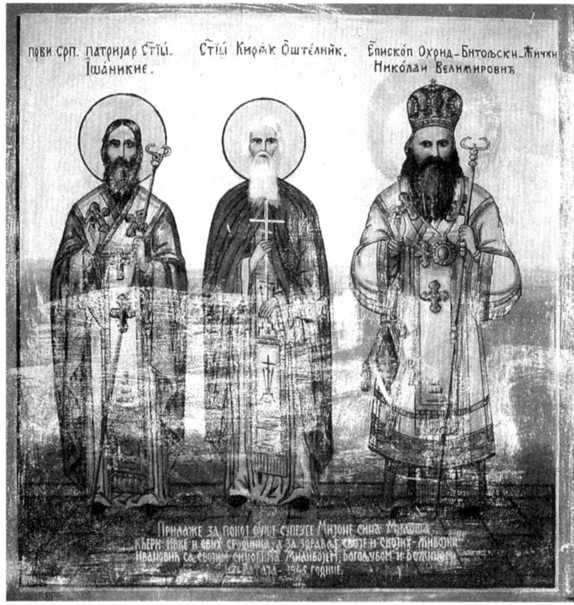

The first fresco of Holy Bishop Nikolai, painted while he was still living
(In the church in Rataj, Alexandar County, painted in 1945)

PART FOUR

Contemporary Testimonies

Metropolitan AMPHILOCHIUS (Radovich)

The Theanthropic Ethos of Bishop Nikolai Velimirovich

Bishop ATHANASIUS (Yevtich)

The Christology of St. Nikolai, Bishop of Ohrid and Zhicha

Bishop IRINEJ (Dobrijevic)

St. Nikolai of Zhicha: A Contemporary Orthodox Witness

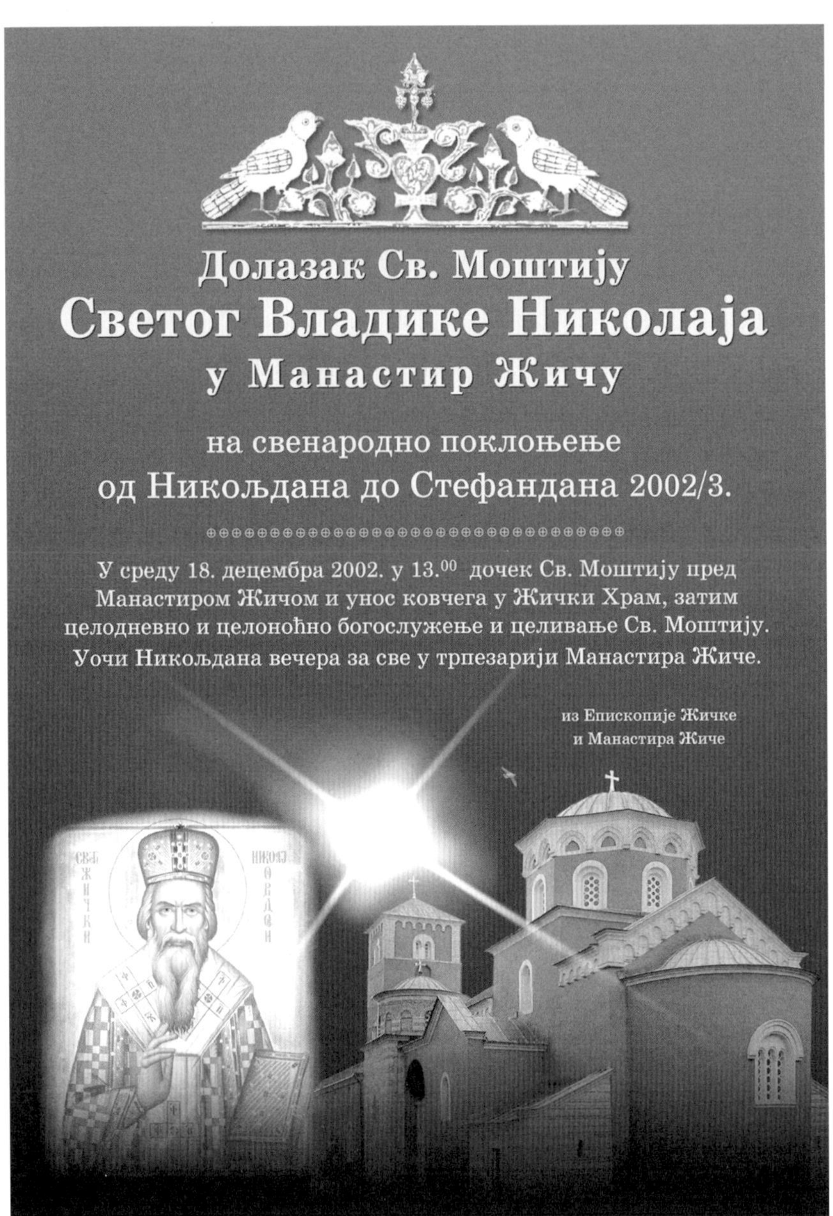

A flyer with information about arrival of Saint Nikolai's holy relics at Zhicha Monastery, 2002–2003

The Theanthropic Ethos of Bishop Nikolai Velimirovich

by Metropolitan Amphilochius (Radovich)

I will say a few words about the theanthropic ethos of Bishop Nikolai. The religious and moral rebirth of the Serbian people is viewed as the theme of Bishop Nikolai's life. And truly, this was the theme that the young Nikolai Velimirovich already presented in his speech at his graduation reception in 1902. He ceaselessly occupied himself with the topic of spiritual and moral rebirth, and this in one way or another remained his theme for more than fifty years, up until his blessed repose. His life and all his labors were dedicated to this theme. His living and life-giving rhetoric and all his writings were directed to this goal. His living word comes not only from contact with the truth of this world and the truth of man, but also from the foundational truth of the Logos, the invisible truth of everything that exists. The person of Christ is that truth, the core of Bishop Nikolai's work and thought. This truth represents that which he served and followed his entire life. This is the truth that gives light to the mind and transfigures the heart of every man coming into the world (cf. John 1:9), both the individual person, and the community. From his youth Bishop Nikolai fled, as he said, "from the deadly conditions in our Church," from the unbearable crises of his time. He felt that the living source of faith among the people had dried up. No one, at the beginning of the twentieth century, felt this crisis of faith in his people as deeply as the young Nikolai Velimirovich. He felt the people of that time (and when he speaks about the people he speaks about everyone who belongs to that people, even those who lead them—their spiritual leaders and their national leaders) were all sinking into indifference. This was the expression that he felt was fit to use for a sermon at that time.

As for the rhetoric of that time, he said that it was a mass of exhausted, impoverished, dry phrases, endlessly repeated. The right word, the word of the Gospel, the word of Truth, he says, should be like thunder.

He spent his entire life searching precisely for such a word, for such a thunderous sermon.

What was characteristic of the young Nikolai was not only his effort for the improvement of rhetoric. He not only followed with the liveliest interest the happenings among his people, the question of unity and unification in all the areas of life, but he also followed all that was happening throughout Europe. Bishop Nikolai was from the very beginning a European man, but one who was pan-Slavically and pan-humanly inclined. He followed the theological, spiritual, scientific and social currents of his time. While living in Switzerland and working on his dissertation *O Hristovom Vaskrsenju* (*On Christ's Resurrection*), he tackled the essential questions of the meaning of life. After living in England in 1908, he would constantly return there, always keeping in contact with that country and with its esteemed people until his death. It is in England that he gave his famous sermons, studied Anglican theology and theologians, wrote about Shakespeare. He maintained a correspondence with Bishop Bell and others until the twilight of his earthly life. Without taking England into account it is difficult to understand his works, his thought, his way of preaching, his method of pastoring his flock, his election to the episcopacy, and especially his activity when he was appointed as the head of the *Bogomoljci* (God-Prayer) Movement. It was through England that he came into contact with India, Hinduism, Brahmanism, and became friends with the great Indian poet Tagore. Many of his writings, beginning with *Reci o Svecoveku* (*Orations on the Universal Man*), are fruits of that encounter, combined with his experience of Orthodoxy as a living Faith that is "above East and West." In America he was an envoy of the Serbian Government during World War I and a missionary of the 1920s; and later, until his repose, he was an exile there. He made dynamic contact with the Episcopal Church of America, even giving sermons in their churches (such as his famous sermon in the Church of Divine Mercy on the topic "To Be or To Do"—"*Biti ili Delati*") and making lifelong friendships with some of their respected people.

We can see from the writings of Bishop Nikolai that he followed the religious currents of his time, the social and societal turmoil in Europe and the world, and scientific research as well. He studied the philosophy of Berkeley and received his doctorate for this; he tackled Nietzsche and Marx (as in his essay *Tri Aveta Evropske Civilizacije—Three Phantoms of European Civilization*). He cautiously followed currents in Roman Catholicism and Protestantism in general, viewing the development of Western Christian churches as a reflection of the peoples whom he at one time considered to be the leaders and examples of culture for the whole world. We, today, are not the first to encounter the problem of Euro-American globalism. Bishop Nikolai had already encountered all the faults and virtues of Euro-centrism. In his first period, he was carried away by Europe's ideas and ideals, but in time would become—especially on the eve of and during World War II—sobered by Nazism and Bolshevism, and he came to comprehend the entire malignity of the European deification of "concupiscence and base intellect." This sobering up, during the second period of his life (which was the result of his encounter with Orthodox Russia, the Ohrid of St. Clement and Naum, and the Holy Mountain of St. Sava and other Athonite Fathers), greatly contributed to his deepening, prayerfully and ascetically, within the living Orthodox tradition of his people, within the Biblical experience and the experience of the Holy Fathers of the Church of Christ.

Bishop Nikolai's words have been preserved about how he would gladly renounce that first period of his life and everything he wrote during that period. But that was an integral part of his life and his persona. That period can be designated as the period of his humanistic religious enthusiasm, from which came *San o Sveslovenskoj Religiji* (*Dream of a pan-Slavic Religion*), *O Svecoveku* (*On the Universal Man*), and *O Jedinstvenom Ekumenskom Hriscanstvu* (*On the Unique Ecumenical Christianity*). He was tied to the reality of the societal currents and messianic enthusiasms of his time, distinctive to Europe and to European intellectual and ecclesiastical circles in the first half of the twentieth century.

It took Bishop Nikolai to be sent to Dachau to fully define Europe as the "White Demonia," as "concupiscence and intellect," and everything else that he wrote in his famous work, written in prison, *Kroz Tamnicki Prozor* (*Through the Prison Window*). While being in constant dialogue with Europe and America, in his first period with them, we can peacefully say that Bishop Nikolai considered himself, especially toward Europe, as a student. Encouraged and inspired by the great ideas of Western Christian nations, he remained to the end of his life loyal to his perception, which was expressed in the above-mentioned sermon, "*Biti ili Delati*" ("To Be or To Do"), where the East is "to be" and the West is "to do." God's is to be *and* to do. That is why only through the unification of being and doing is it possible to find a balance between the human being and human history. Not even in his later years did Bishop Nikolai cease his relations with the West, especially with people with whom he had developed friendships from the very beginning—specifically from 1916, when the book *George Bell and Nikolai* by Muriel Heppell was printed in English. This correspondence between Bishop Nikolai and the Anglican Bishop is a valuable testimony about him. Equally interesting was the friendship between Bishop Nikolai and Episcopalian Bishop of New York, Manning. Nikolai's relationship with him and his attendance at his funeral in the Cathedral of St. John the Divine in New York will be remembered, as will the first icon of Nikolai, which was painted by an Anglican bishop and is kept in the same cathedral. At the same time, it should be stressed that Bishop Nikolai, in his mature period, in the wartime and postwar time, did not behave as a student toward Europe but rather as a *prophet,* who, in the spirit of the Old Testament prophets, felt responsible for not only for his people but for all the people of Europe and the world without exception.

Bishop Nikolai was one of the rare apostles of the twentieth century, who felt responsible for all peoples and nations. In this sense he was an evangelical man more than any of his contemporaries. Schooled by his Serbian people whom God entrusted to him, he learned love toward all people and all creation. Therefore, to reduce Nikolai to the level of some national bard would be a great sin against him. Bishop Nikolai's personality was too immense and too complex for it to be condensed into any earthly equation or size. This is what many Serbs overlook. They especially overlook it when they view him through the defective and superficially understood prism of *Nebeska Srbija* (*Heavenly Serbia*), identifying him with chauvinism, absolutist nationalism, exclusiveness, and introversion into his biological existence, as it is said nowadays. Bishop Nikolai was and remains a great preacher of universal horizons, a philosopher, theologian, pedagogue, a rare wise-man and poet. At the very least he discovered the mystery of the greatest and universal One. In the universal, cosmic and super-cosmic he discovered the meaning of the smallest, of those who at first glance are the most insignificant. His wisdom and love were incarnated in everything: equally in a worm under the bark of a bush, in the constellations, or in pan-human existence. His care touched the invisible atom, the most despised creature, especially those who are most despised and lowliest among men. His care and love were pan-human care and love. We are not wrong if we say that Europe in the twentieth century, not just our Serbian people, did not beget another man like him, who merged within himself to such a degree love toward his people and his little village of Lelich with pan-human nature and being. As a truly godly man, he realized and achieved a balance between the individual and the general, the material and spiritual, God and man, national and pan-human. He was able to succeed in doing this through the mystery of Christ, the Only Lover of man, as he called Him in one of his final works, in the mystery of the Christ's Orthodox Church.

Encountering India and its ancient wisdom in England, he absorbed within himself that wisdom of the Far East. His famous works such as *Reci o Svecoveku (Orations on the Universal Man), Molitve na Jezeru (Prayers by the Lake), Indijska Pisma (Indian Letters), Iznad Istoka i Zapada (Above East and West)* and other works show how he delved and immersed himself into that wisdom of the Far East. He did this for his sake, for his people's sake, especially for the sake of those in his intellectual environment who were always inclined to be enchanted by the foreign; he did this for the sake of the possibility of bearing witness to Christ before the peoples of the Far East. Sensing India as the Serbian and pan-Slavic ancient homeland, he was connected to it and her mystical experience of pan-cosmism and pan-divinity.

His sense of apostolic responsibility for all people and all nations can be explained. It is a fact that he was nearly the first Christian bishop who preached Christ, in English, in the 20s of the twentieth century, to African Americans in Manhattan, New York.[1] As a witness of the true Gospel and as Christ's Apostle, he communicated with occupying soldiers during World War II and with SS officers in Dachau. From this we can rightfully say that the heart of Bishop Nikolai was a national heart, in the original meaning of the word, and simultaneously a pan-human heart. He acquired it by listening to the beating pulse and heart of his Christian people, expanded it by following for a time the principles of European humanistic people, and made it infinite by meeting with the Person of the Only Lover of Man, Who represents the greatest possible perfection that a man can have on earth: an encounter founded on the experience of the Church of the East, the Orthodox Church, the Church of St. Sava's

[1] St. Philip's Church in Harlem, New York.—TRANS.

people. It was in no way an accident that one of his first works was *Reci of Svecoveku (Orations on the Universal Man)*, and his final work was *Jedini Covekoljubac (The Only Lover of Man)*. Fr. Radovan Bigich, in his doctoral work at the Theological University,[2] defined Nikolai's life path exceptionally well with the title: *Od Svecoveka do Bogocoveka (From the Universal Man to the God-man)*.

Truly, Bishop Nikolai moved on his life's path from the Universal Man (i.e., the universal and pan-religious experience and sense and humanistic-European pan-unity), walking step by step, deeper and deeper, so that in the end he would reach the Person of the God-man. Hence it is possible, without a doubt, to speak about his theanthropic ethos, about the theanthropic nature of his persona, about his creativity and his overall works.

The life path of Bishop Nikolai was a dramatic one; it was a path of organic maturation. His life experience and the experience of Fr. Justin (Popovich) were in their depths the same; nonetheless, the journey of Fr. Justin was different from the journey of Bishop Nikolai, his teacher. It is possible that Fr. Justin's journey was different precisely because Bishop Nikolai's preceded it. Bishop Nikolai was the first to tackle his drama and the existential crucifixions of himself and his time; he suffered through and experienced, in his own skin, the tragedy, doubt, and divisions of his era, for the sake of Fr. Justin and for many other of his contemporaries. That is why Fr. Justin, even from his first writings (1916), showed stability and unwaveringness in faith, and why he was crystal clear in bearing witness and giving testimony, and remained like this until the end of his life. His path was not ascending and gradual like it was for Bishop Nikolai; rather, it was a descending walk into the depths. That which he started, he only built upon. Bishop Nikolai did this as well, but he was very different in style and in language. This is the beauty of the Church of God and of the people of God who are poured into Her theanthropic image-foundry. In the Church, everyone has their own path which they take; but what is important is how the path is completed and what a human life is filled with at the end. Nikolai's universal religiosity and morality, having assumed form in the person of the God-man, did not mean that his pan-humanity and Universal Man became narrow, like many people of limited intellect, or, as I usually say, "with a fly's memory" think and

[2] Belgrade Theological University.—TRANS.

say. People like these think that the humanistic perception of man, the world, and God is more expansive and more encompassing than the perception of man, the world, and God which is formed on the foundation of the Person of the God-man. It is the complete opposite: pan-humanity and the Universal Man receive, in the God-man, their true Name which is above every name. Those who live in the God-man receive their ability to exist as persons, their depth and infiniteness, and their common denominator, freeing themselves from impersonal cosmopolitanism and from drowning in the impersonal and the abstract, which inevitably results in drowning in nothingness. The all-encompassing and infinite super-intellectual Image of the Only Lover of Man, Who through Himself reveals the Holy Trinitarian mystery of being and existence, Who through Himself manifests it and Who through Himself bears witness to it, represents the inexpressible Fullness of Him Who fills all in all (Apostle Paul—Eph. 1:21–22, Col. 2:9–10).

Phthisical minds accuse Bishop Nikolai of nationalism, others again of anti-Semitism. By this, both of them only show that they are too immature to engage in polemics with this titan of spirit and wisdom. Such spiritual midgets, ignoramuses with conceited minds of darkened consciousnesses and consciences, are not capable of sailing off into the depths of Nikolai's person and works. They are burdened with self-love or with some other idol and mask of universalism and false humanism; or, possibly, with hidden hatred and disdain toward all peoples on earth like the "goyim," except one nation; such people find in others that which they carry within themselves. They don't even know what truly divine and truly human love is. Bishop Nikolai's thought is founded in God as in eternal Love, in the Holy Trinity, in the Mystery of the incarnation of God and in His inexpressible love of man (see: *Cassiana)*. Such a thought does not know nor is able to know or recognize any borders or limits of this Love. Only one border exists that slices through every human heart, and that border is between light and darkness, good and evil, life and death.

Bishop Nikolai's love of man is not an abstract love of man but rather real love-of-man. In Christ's Person both commandments are realized: Love the Lord God with all your heart, and love your neighbor as you love yourself. Whoever loves the true God, loves the true man. Learn the true love-of-God and the true love-of-man. The love-of-Christ is the true love-of-God and the true love-of-man. When knowing the perfect God in Christ and the perfect man, we know how/who/what we need to love in God, man, and in every people. From the love that is realized toward the closest of our neighbors, we learn true love toward every creature, every human being, near or far. For love to be true, it needs to be checked by the relationship toward one's closest neighbor. If it does not mature in one's relationship toward the closest of neighbors, man, nation, and creation, then it will never become true and unselfish love. If it is not there for those who are closest, how will it become true love for those who are far, even if it is for some faraway star, or some man who belongs to another nationality or some other continent, or if it is for some different nationality? Love toward one's neighbors, toward one's family and people, represents a school of love toward every man, every people; a school for pan-human and theanthropic love.

Bishop Nikolai loved his people with unselfish love. It is precisely because he loved them, that from his youth he rebuked their faults and weaknesses. Exactly like the biblical Prophets. If we were to measure Bishop Nikolai against his bitter and terse words, which he spoke and wrote about his people many times, and against that with which he rebuked and how he rebuked, he would be proclaimed as the greatest Serb-hater and anti-Serb among the Serbian people in their history. It is precisely that rebuke of evil in the Serbian people, their errors and wandering off from the path, that reveals he indeed loved them deeply. His relationship with his people is one of a prophet. This Prophetic dimension of his persona and his love, especially in his more mature years, is a key to what he wrote and spoke about his people and as well as about Europe and Jews. No one loved the chosen people of God, the Jews, as much as did their Prophets. Moreover, anyone who is at least familiar with the Prophetic Books will know that no one has so radically rebuked that nation, their faults and shortcomings, especially their apostasy from God, as their Prophets had so precisely done. Let us take for example the Prophets Isaiah and Jeremiah, or any other great and minor Prophet, or let us look at Prophet Elijah (Elias) in his own time. Are we going to call them, the Prophets of God, anti-Semites and haters of their own people because of their rebukes? Or are we actually talking about people, and indeed we are, who possess in themselves a great love of God, Who chastises exactly because He loves. In like manner, the Apostle Paul, a Jew, of the Jewish nation, was prepared to lose his soul and his salvation, in order to save his people

(Rom. 9:15). That same Apostle Paul called his people "dogs" (Phil. 3:2), not due to hatred toward them, but rather in order to sober them up and bring them to God and eternal enlightenment in Christ. Bishop Nikolai is of the same caliber. It is in that Prophetic spirit that we should understand everything terse and bitter that he wrote about his Serbian people, about Europe, and about the people of Israel.

Bishop Nikolai was a man of enormous love toward every creature and every being. The way he loved his mother—and he loved her with his whole heart and soul—is the way he loved everyone, every human being, every creature, and felt indebted not only to his people but to every nation and to every man. This can be seen not only in his writings and on the basis of his written wisdom, but primarily from his personal relationship toward everyone he met, not taking into account which nation they belonged to. We can see evidence of this in his behavior toward the people in England, and in America, where he completed his earthly life. This is evident by the fact of the great respect he deservedly enjoyed from the most intelligent people of his time across Europe, America, and even people from the Far East.

It was his fellow countrymen that dragged him through mud the most and continue to do so. Like the words of the Gospel say: *He came to His own, and His own did not receive Him* (John 1:11). Elsewhere in the Gospels it is written: *A prophet is not without honor except in his own county* (Matt. 13:57).

Bishop Nikolai was a man of the Gospel, for whom the border between people, states, and nations did not exist; and he cared in a pan-human and theanthropic manner for every creature and every living being. Because of this, he was aware of the enormous responsibility and role in history, positive and negative, of the first chosen people of God; he was aware of the good which they bear and of the great danger that their estrangement from God causes to themselves and to the whole world. Bishop Nikolai at times, in relating to them, uses Prophetic language, not rebuking them out of hatred toward them but out of a deep, Christ-like and Christ-inspired love and care for their deliverance and salvation. We have to understand his bitter and terse words about Europe in the same way, as if they were directed at his own people. It is within this context that we need to understand his basic concept and vision of the history of the Old and New Israel, and of overall humanity.

Bishop Nikolai, alongside all of the seeming inconsistencies in his life, remained consistent to himself, to the thirst he had from his youth for the truth and the meaning of life, to his first vision, to the first encounter with the Divine mystery which was, in the beginning, not clearly defined and visible enough. That was the vision which, in his words, he had stumbled upon and grasped in the snake-pit of this world—the Person of Christ the God-man, the Only Lover of man. Having grasped Him once, he never let Him go, so that after the hell of Dachau and his journey through it, he would leave a testimony that while he was in there he, like the patriarch Jacob of old, *saw God*; and for that reason he no longer believed in Him, but *knew and recognized* Him. Maturing more deeply in God-seeing and love, he began to love all people, all nations, and all of creation through that God-seeing love. He loved them with that love with which God loved and loves the world from its inception and before it.

This theanthropic love, which is the living pulse of the life and works of the Bishop of Ohrid, Zhicha, and all America, Nikolai, represents that which made him and makes him an Apostle of Christ, a contemporary Apostle not only among his Serbian people, but also an Apostle of Europe, America, and the entire world. It is the same kind of Apostle that Christ wanted His first disciples to be, and how His first Apostles and the Apostles of the Church of Christ throughout the ages were.

Having inadequately displayed a few grains of the extremely rich treasure of the wisdom of Bishop Nikolai, I will add the following at the end: It is truly a great and blessed thing that his relics have found their way to his Zhicha. I would whisper something more which some might find unfavorable, but which is completely logical and natural: Bishop Nikolai, only after St. Sava, has glorified Zhicha the most, and he belongs to it. Bishop Nikolai should stay here in Zhicha, and with his relics and persona he should continue his Apostolic work and his work in the style of St. Sava!

Metropolitan of Montenegro
and the Coastlands, Amphilochius
Translated by Radomir Plavsic

The Christology of St. Nikolai, Bishop of Ohrid and Zhicha

by Bishop Athanasius (Yevtich)

The wise King Solomon, in his beautiful Book of Wisdom, expounds on the Eternal Wisdom of God: *Being but one, she can do all things; and, remaining in herself, she maketh all things new; and in all ages, entering into holy souls, she maketh them friends of God, and prophets* (Wis. 7:27).

Those whose hearts are open to divine wisdom, planted in men and in all creation, are friends of the Wisdom of God. Those people endowed by God with wisdom since birth are sages, philosophers by nature, who then nurture that wisdom through arduous learning and acquisition of knowledge, and further it through life experience and the personal experience of the Wisdom of God within themselves, in others, and in all of God's creation. Though in this way they may become the friends of God, it is still not enough to make them the *prophets* of God, as wise Solomon remarks. Only the hypostatic Wisdom of God—Christ, the Eternal Logos and Son of the All-wise God—can make them prophets.

We know that what is called in the Old Testament the "Wisdom of God" is Christ, "the power of God and **Wisdom** of God," as the holy Apostle Peter says in the New Testament (1 Cor 1:24). Therefore, only those who by innate natural wisdom and with acquired, cultured human philosophy, attain the Eternal Wisdom of God—incarnate and actualized in Jesus Christ, the Lord and Savior of men and the world—only those become true *Friends* and *Prophets* of God. Such were the apostles and the prophets, and with them and after them the Holy Fathers of Christ's Church throughout ages. Such was in our time, in the twentieth century, Bishop Nikolai Velimirovich, Bishop of Ohrid and Zhicha, and today's Symposium is dedicated to his work and person.

⁘ ⁘ ⁘

Nikolai undoubtedly was such a God-gifted, truly *wise man*, naturally so—but he was also an accomplished *philosopher* and *theologian* whose philosophical and theological proportions and range cannot be denied, whether we accept or reject his philosophy and theology. Nikolai remained such until the end of his life on earth. But this is only half the truth about Bishop Nikolai—the other, more important part of his personality and work is exactly that other part mentioned by wise Solomon. The nature of wisdom, although stemming from the same divine source, is not sufficient to indeed become a genuine and a personal acquaintance and a *friend* and a *prophet* of God. It was made possible and realized only when the Wisdom of God Himself, in the Person of Christ, voluntary and in flesh, came to the world and united with those (philosophers) who longed for wisdom. It is through this relation, communion and closeness that they become essentially God-like and Christ-like *friends* and God-inspired *prophets* "of the Spirit of Wisdom: the Understanding Spirit, Holy, Only Begotten, Lover of the good, Almighty, Overseer of all things" (πανεπίσκοπον, all-seeing); the Wisdom that is the "Pure Image of the Glory of the Sustainer of the World, the Radiance of the Eternal Holiness, the Image of His Goodness." (Wis. 7:22–26; Heb. 1:3–6; Col. 1:15; 2 Cor. 4:4; Phil. 2:16).

All these characteristics of the Wisdom of God, as was observed by the wise Solomon, pertain directly to Christ, the Logos and Wisdom of God, the Creator of Wisdom, men, and all creation. For there is no other Wisdom, some different Sophia (a newfangled fantasy of a few Russian philosophizing theologians, i.e., *Sophiologists*—Soloviev, Florensky, Bulgakov, Berdyaev) apart from and without Christ, by which people themselves can become wise, learn how to philosophize, or acquire the mind of God. Christ is therefore the key to all Nikolai's wisdom and philosophy, for Nikolai, even before becoming a Bishop, and especially after becoming the Bishop of Ohrid and Zhicha, in truth met Christ and clung to Him with all his heart and mind, with all his soul and with all his strength (cf. Matt. 22:37). For he loved Him and followed His footsteps all his life, like a sheep that followed its Shepherd—or more precisely, like a martyr (witness) of the Lamb of God, he followed Him wherever He went. It was His Eternal Gospel that Nikolai carried and fervently preached throughout his whole life (cf. Rev. 14:4,6, 7:13–17).

This is by no means some apodictic, preconceived conclusion, but the result of our modest (nonetheless persistent) research of Bishop Nikolai, his personality and work, and especially his literary works.[1] There are numerous texts not yet published and it is our intent to try and shed some light on those during the course of this lecture.

On Nikolai's *journey to Christ* or, more accurately, his following after Christ, he never vacillated or blundered, but searched, and searched always all the more deeply, painstakingly, and with his entire being he looked for and followed in the footsteps of the Cosmic Traveler throughout all of creation. Nonetheless, he searched especially in the *realm* of our own being, or—as St. Maximus the Confessor said—in our souls and bodies, and then in nature and history, and along the paths he took in his lifetime and personal struggles experienced during the journey. The Cosmic Traveler often eludes us on this journey by deliberately hiding and escaping from us in order to make us look for Him with our whole hearts and minds, following farther and deeper after Him, following after His *footsteps* and the sweet scent of His *myrrh*—images which poignantly allude to those in the *Song of Songs*.

Some critics have described this search as the *development* of his thought, or the evolution of his theology. We would rather employ the terminology used by the Apostle Paul in saying that the word of God *increased*, and "mightily *grew* among the faithful" (cf. Acts 6:7, 19:20), "when the faith is *increased*" (cf. 2 Cor. 10:15), and "all over the world this gospel is *bearing fruit* and *growing*" (cf. Col. 1:6, 2:19), and that "we will in all things *grow up* into him Who is the Head, that is, Christ. From him the whole body, joined and held together by every supporting ligament, *grows* and *builds itself up* in love..." (cf. Eph. 4: 15–16). The Apostle Peter uses the same language in his second epistle: *But grow in grace and in the knowledge of our Lord and Savior Jesus Christ* (2 Pet. 3:18). Similar expressions are employed by St. Basil the Great when he speaks of "growing into faith," as he writes of himself:

[1] It was by God's will and completely undeservedly that I came across thirty of Bishop Nikolai's notebooks, which include essays and commentary on figures like Njegosh and Dostoyevsky. These begin as early as 1941 (though most date from the post-war period, after his move to the United States), and are mainly written in Serbian, with occasional English and even Russian entries. I carried some of these notebooks across the Yugoslav border secretly, hidden in my undershirt, because of the risk that, being brought from abroad and especially because they were by Nikolai, they would be confiscated by the Communists. I received most of them from Bishop Dionysius (Milivojevic) of the American-Canadian Diocese, who took them from Nikolai's room in South Canaan, Pennsylvania.

> If other things in me may move a sigh, this one boast at least I dare make in the Lord, that never for one moment have I held erroneous conceptions about God, or entertained heterodox opinions, which I have learnt later to change (τήν ἔννοιαν... αὐξηθεῖσαν)... On my coming to ripe years of reason I did not shift my opinions from one to another, but *carried out* (ἐτελείωσα) the principles (τάς ἀρχάς) delivered to me by my parents. Just as the seed when it *grows* is first tiny and then gets bigger but always preserves its identity, not changed in kind though gradually *perfected in growth*, so I reckon the same doctrine to have *grown* in my case through gradually advancing stages... Has there been the slightest want of harmony in my utterances about the faith at Chalcedon, again and again at Heraclea, and at an earlier period in the suburb of Cæsarea? Are they not all mutually consistent? I only except the *increase in force* of which I spoke just now, resulting from advance, and which is not to be regarded as a change from worse to better, but rather as *a filling up* of what was wanting in the addition of knowledge.
>
> (*Against Eustathius of Sebaste, Letter 223*:3–5; comp. *Letter 259*:2 and *Letter 125*:3)

Everything written by Nikolai was done with sincerity of mind and heart, and he was a exceptionally gifted thinker and prolific writer with a warm, compassionate soul. For that reason I first thought of giving a lecture entitled "Nikolai, a Wise Man by Nature and a Theologian by God's Grace," for he truly was both. A wise man and a philosopher by nature, endowed from early childhood with the gifts of God that he later multiplied as very few have managed to do, he then continued to grow and developed to become a theologian following the best tradition of the Church Fathers. It is evident that he read and pondered quite a bit, but it is also clear that he prayed even more, opening his heart and mind to God, thereby receiving the enlightenment and inspiration of the Holy Spirit. Aside from being highly gifted and apart from the education he received in secular sciences, philosophy, and theology, he also profoundly and sincerely contemplated human nature, deeply and genuinely perceiving life with all its complexities in the same manner he claimed was done by his Serbian people who "did not learn the Bible from books but from life itself."

He learned the Bible through life experience and labors; that is, he learned the Holy Gospel of Christ. Nikolai's love for Christ and His Gospel is evident from his early youth even though, in the beginning, he occasionally emphasized the Gospel as being the *science* of Christ, and then treating as next [in importance] the Person of Christ. Already in 1902, when he delivered his graduation speech at the School of Theology, the young Nikolai said, "The science of the God-man is still as fresh and powerful as it was when He first preached it to the world from the Mount of Olives." Two years later Nikolai wrote about the "agelessness of the Gospel's ideas," but still connected its knowledge and ideas with the Person of Christ. Examples of this can be found in his 1904 essay "The God-man in Jerusalem," or in his 1909 doctoral thesis on the Resurrection of Christ, as well as in a text on "The Gospel of Resurrection" where he says:

> We would be greatly mistaken in concluding that Jesus of Nazareth's systematic teachings alone opened the door to the glorious and victorious spread of Christianity... This was accomplished before all else by the very fact of His Resurrection, from which everything else acquires meaning.

It is also worth noting Nikolai's early commentary on Njegosh's Christology:

> [It] is almost rudimentary... Nevertheless, even in this rudimentary Christology one can find the basic elements of the Church's Christology. Christ is the Son of the "Pre-Eternal Father," Who, incarnate (*Who put on human nature*), came to this world to bring justice and enlightenment, to destroy idolatry with His teaching, to defeat death with His Resurrection—therefore all world celebrates Him as its Savior.
>
> (From "The Theology of Njegosh" in his study *The Religion of Njegosh*, 1910.)

In his text "On Restoring the Dignity of Body," also from 1910, he writes: "Christianity has bestowed new dignity on our bodies by teaching about the *Incarnation* of our God and the *Resurrection* of Christ from the dead." Some time later, in 1916, in his chapter on Tolstoy (*The Religious Spirit of the Slavs: Slav Orthodoxy*) he writes in a characteristic manner about the Person of Christ:

> Tolstoy exalted only Christ's Sermon on the Mount—that is, only Christ's teaching, or part of Christ's teaching. The Orthodox Church exalted Christ Himself... The Church thought there was something greater than Christ's words—Christ Himself. His words are extraordinary, it is true—He spoke as no man ever spoke before—but His person and His life were more extraordinary still.

It was therefore appropriately and rightly remarked by Djordje Janic in his study on Bishop Nikolai that "during the sixty years of his fighting for Christ, [he] remained within the framework of Orthodox teaching" and did not go astray from the Orthodoxy of the Holy Fathers.[2]

It should also be said that Nikolai's early Christology closely resembles that of early Christian writers, especially the Apologists, among whom we number St. Justin the Philosopher, Theophilus of Antioch and Clement of Alexandria. It can be best described as the Christology of the Logos, a distinct cosmological and humanistic Christology which is not altogether wrong, but incomplete and one-sided, permeated mainly by philosophical-apologetic thought rather than theological-liturgical or ecclesiastical understanding. Examples of this are numerous. In his book of sermons *Beyond Sin and Death*" (a sermon entitled "Christ Walks Slowly," 1914) he writes:

[2] Djordje Janic writes: "If we carefully examine Nikolai's spiritual and philosophical maturation and the Bishop's intellectual and spiritual development, if we follow closely his thought from its inception, the contradictions and inconsistencies—allegedly apparent when interpreting certain themes—suddenly disappear. During the battle he fought for the Lord for over sixty years, he remained firmly in the Orthodox faith. In many aspects he came close to the ways of the early Christians, the Apostles and Church Fathers, who introduced every day life into theology, who not only lived by it but also with it. His texts often remind us of what we read in the Old Testament Prophets or the sermons of St. John Chrysostom. From his school days until the end of his life, the bishop longed to see Christianity return to the path indicated by Lord—that is, that we live only by God. Christ was to become again the way of life for every Christian. He would not only be on everyone's tongue, but in everyone's heart and deed. The Light from the Cross dispersed all burdens and temptations of the culture, making for him room, together with Fr. Justin Popovich, in the center of Serbian spirituality. In any year, be it 1900 or 1912 or 1917 or 1923 or 1939 or 1945 or 1956, Nikolai remained with the same thoughts in whose core was Jesus Christ. The nation and community were his only other interests" (*Hadji into Eternity* [Belgrade, 1994], pp. 5, 7, 22, 23, 27, 28, 32).

> Christ is dearest and closest to God the Father... This is the fundamental premise by which people live. Without it the world would lapse back into its original chaos... Christ! That name became the synthesis of all the noblest ideals of this world. Freedom, reason, love, faith, labor—all can be found in a single name: Christ... God builds a house (the world) of which Christ is the foundation and all men are bricks.

And in a lecture delivered in London in 1920, he says:

> What was Christianity like in the beginning? In the beginning it was our Lord Jesus Christ Himself. Who was Jesus Christ? He was the fulfillment and realization of God's laws and prophecies... But that is not all. Christ came as the fulfillment of all God's laws and promises made to many nations through various prophets. This is how He unified and fulfilled the holy laws of numerous religions and civilizations from the beginning of history. When the fulfillment of the Law occurred in Judaism, it simultaneously occurred in all the divine laws in Hinduism, Buddhism, Taoism, Zoroastrianism, Druidism, in the religious systems of Egypt and Greece. In a word, it was a fulfillment of all that had been divine in all religions, from the most primitive to the most sophisticated... It is not my intent to confuse Christianity with idolatry—God forbid! Perish the thought! I am far from the thought of denying the divine perfection of the Person of Christ, and that by introducing some new teachings from different religions I am attempting to concoct a new Creed. God forbid it should ever be! Christ is the eternal Wisdom of God. From the beginning of the world the Wisdom of God had been shedding gleams of His Light on many nations; so when the time came, the Wisdom of God became incarnate as the Divine Person Jesus Christ and came to dwell among men on earth. Only this time not as a ray of sunlight but as the Sun Himself—the Source of all light. Christ came by assuming human flesh, not by being born again... For Christ is not some artificial creation made up of different attributes, but the complete and most perfect Divine Person.
>
> (*The Spiritual Rebirth of Europe*, *CW*, vol. 3, pp. 746–48)

It should be clear from the above passages, and there are numerous such passages available from that period, that even then Nikolai was with Christ ("I would follow Christ even if all others renounced Him"—*Sermons at the Foot of the Mount*, 1912—a very similar statement appears in Dostoevsky), but the Christian apologist in him is still active with all its cosmological-anthropological and philosophical-religious elements. We find here an explanation for the short-lived enthusiasm Nikolai expressed for panhumanism—that is, the idea of Universal Man. Many, including Nikolai, recognized Christ in this ideal, but this was a cosmological and anthropological, even anthropocentric Christ rather than the living God-man and the Savior preached in the Gospels and preached by the Church. It is not the purpose of this lecture to draw attention to this, since it does not represent a complete picture of Nikolai in his true light. Suffice it to say that elements of such a Christology can be found even in his *Prayers by the Lake*. But who can judge or evaluate a poet and a philosopher? (In his *Orations on the Universal Man*, already written in 1917, and published anonymously in 1920, we find an indication that Nikolai does not stand behind all of his work—and what we deal with here is a polemic work of Nikolai who is expressing his view on Nietzsche's Superman in a poetic-philosophical form). According to the Church Fathers, the views of Church writers expressed in an apologetic-polemic manner are not to be placed on equal footing as those dealing with dogmatic-theological writing—writers of poetry and polemic have recourse to ideas and language that would be unjustifiable and unpalatable if used in theological treatises.[3] Likewise, our attitude toward practitioners of each genre should reflect these relative standards.

At any rate, Nikolai overcame some difficulties that surfaced during his research and examination. He had overcome his philosophical-apologetic approach to the overwhelming Mystery of Christ, and going forward he expressed in his writing a fully Orthodox Christology as taught by the Church Fathers. It is interesting to compare, for example, his *Prayers by the Lake* from 1923 to the *Akathist to Christ the Conqueror of Death*, written immediately after, and see his theological and spiritual growth and his full Christology.

⁂

[3] Examples include St. Athanasius the Great (*On Dionysius of Alexandria*) and St. Photius of Constantinople (*The Bibliotheca* and *The Letter to the Armenians*).

A very similar situation occurred with Nikolai's interest in the questions of Ecclesiology that also led to his involvement with *Ecumenism*, or, as Bishop Amphilochius said, with the question of "bringing the Churches together." In his shorter works, written before World War I, we find some questionable statements from the young hieromonk Nikolai in relation to the unification of all Christian denominations. Even though Nikolai always remained with Christ and His True Church, his Christology and Ecclesiology in this early period seem to be incomplete. He says, for instance, "I always believe in the ultimate victory of Christ" (*The Slave Uprising*, 1917), because "Jesus of Nazareth was the Son of God, the co-eternal Person of the Holy Trinity" (*The Agony of the Church*, ch. 1; *The Wisdom of the Church*, 1917). In some other works from that time (*The Drama of the Church*, 1917, etc.) he closely links Christ and the Church: His life and her life; His drama (that is, the Passion) and the dramatic suffering of the Church in the world and history. Even when he talks about the "unification of churches," he talks about the struggle of the Church for the true exposition of faith ("The Church had to stand against the false teachings of the heretics for her sake, and correct them for their sake" [*Collected Works (CW),* vol. 3, pp. 111–12]).

It should be admitted, though, that in writings from this early period he reveals a somewhat weak knowledge of the Church Fathers and their theology of the true faith and the true Church. In his characteristic way, he writes,

> The Christian Church is a *Christocracy*... Theocracy (in the Church) has never been accepted because it was not at the same time *Christocracy* and *Hagiocracy*. The Saints are infallible only in Christ... It is not we people [who are perfect] but Christ in us Who is infallible.

These words also clearly demonstrate Nikolai's opinion that the Roman Catholic Church's teachings [regarding Papal infallibility] are false, an opinion he would reiterate with greater frequency in his later works. It seems that at first he was particularly tolerant and mild in his criticism of the Anglican and other Protestant denominations. His essay "The Question of the Unification of Churches" from 1909 pertains mainly to the unification of the Anglican and Orthodox Churches, but the text has little depth when it comes to the discussion of ecclesiastical matters; he emphasizes only love and [has little to say regarding] the theology of Church. He assumes a similar position in 1915, and only a few years later ("The Victory of the Church," chap. 7 in *The Agony of the Church*, 1917) clearly expresses the Orthodox stand with respect to the ideal of church unification:

> We must return to the only source of Christian strength and majesty—to the spirit of Christ. This rebirth and the revival of Christianity are possible only in a united Church of Christ. This unity is possible only if built on the foundations of the original Church.
>
> (*CW*, vol 3, p. 128 [in Serbian])[4]

In other words, Nikolai even then believed first in Christ and only then that Christ shall unite all Christian nations. Nowhere does he deny the authenticity and uniqueness of the Eastern Orthodox Church, nor does he consider her lacking or defective in any way; rather, in the context of the wartime drama encompassing his and other European nations, he sincerely wished for the unification of all Christian European communities for their benefit and for the benefit of other Christians in the world.[5]

[4] Vasilii Zenkovsky, a Russian theologian and philosopher from Paris, wrote a review about Nikolai's *The Agony of the Church* (the book has four chapters: 1. *The Wisdom of the Church*, 2. *The Drama of the Church*, 3. *The Agony of the Church,* and 4. *The Victory of the Church*), published in London, 1917. He applauds Nikolai's criticism of Europe's abandonment of Christ. Nikolai holds the European Churches mostly responsible for this, as well as for exchanging the "universal spirit of Christ" for the causes of "nationalism and imperialism." However, Zenkovsky disapproves of Nikolai's "offering mainly a theocratic way of Christian life" which is foreign to the spirit of liberty in Christ, and for drawing too close to "Catholic imperialism," the main culprit responsible for the crisis of Western culture. The "Orthodox way," according to Zenkovsky, is unique because only from within can we find the foundation for the unification of churches, only by transforming historic tumults from within and in the "fullness of Orthodoxy."

[5] Nikolai's devotion to the Eastern Orthodox Church is clearly expressed in, for example, his speech at the meeting of the Anglican-Orthodox Society on December 16, 1919, convened in the Cathedral of St. Paul in London (in English, with three additional texts: *The Spiritual Rebirth of Europe* [London, 1920]), when he talked about the "principles of the Eastern Orthodox Church," first praising the Church of St. Sophia in Constantinople, and then what the principle of infallibility in the Eastern Church consists in: "No human is infallible; it is the Ecumenical Council that represents all (local) Christian Churches and is guided by the Holy Spirit. This principle of infallibility has been present in the East throughout our entire history." He then emphasizes "the Or-

Let us now more closely examine Nikolai's Christology from 1922 onwards, from his Ohrid/Mount Athos period, when he was transferred to the Diocese of Ohrid, paying particular attention to his *Prayers by the Lake* and the *Akathist to Christ the Conqueror of Death*. At the beginning of his *Prayers by the Lake* (1922) he chooses as his motto the following: "*You are God Who descended into hell and smashed the iron chains of the slaves*"—meaning that he personally confesses Christ as his Savior using the language of the Orthodox Church. It is clear that these words are

thodox principle of inclusiveness," which has been "in the prayers of the Christian East for the unification of all Christians." Nikolai then continued with the question: "Perhaps it would remain unclear why the Eastern Church wishes for the unification of all Christians when she includes all their specific and specifically formulated principles?"—and he presents three reasons, the first being: *love* of the Eastern Church for all Christians; the second: the state of the world after the First World War; the third: "the white race and Christianity in Europe gravely endangered by the non-Christian nations" because Russia "the strongest link between Europe and Asia is broken." The fate of the white race and Christianity depends on whether Russia is saved or lost. "My voice is the voice of the Christian East crying for the unification of Churches" (*CW*, vol. 3, pp. 757–61). It is interesting that this makes Nikolai the precursor of the other Orthodox appeals, such as *the Encyclical* of the Patriarchate of Constantinople from 1920, calling all Christians to *fellowship* = κοινωνία, that is, the League of Churches (modeled after the League of Nations). Nikolai later also participated, between the two wars, in the ecumenical meetings in Yugoslavia and Europe and the World Council of Churches in Evanston, USA, 1945, of which he provides details (*CW*, vol. 13, pp. 42–46): "In Evanston, one name brought all together and closer—Jesus Christ"; he continues: "The definite resolution was not of theological but of social character... A declaration of the Orthodox representatives points out that every Christian denomination holds only one segment of Christian faith; only the Orthodox Church has the fullness of true faith that was once and for all given unto the Saints (Jude 3)... The real unity of all churches cannot be achieved by mutual concessions, but only by the adoption of the only true faith in its entirety, such as was passed down by the Apostles and formulated at the Councils; in other words, by the return of all Christians to this unique and undivided Church that the ancestors of all Christians belonged to for the first ten centuries after Christ. This true church is the Holy Orthodox Church... When it comes to the questions of principles of faith and the idea of Church, the Orthodox have neither need nor right to change their position... The Orthodox Church is neither left nor right." Nikolai never deviated from the basic principles of Orthodoxy, from ancient Apostolic Orthodox Christianity. There is no time now to expand on his understanding of Orthodox ecumenism. Nikolai criticized Europe even then—that is, civilization without Christ. The same was true for India; the more he learned about her tradition the more critical he became. This resulted in his final criticism of India in his work *The Serbian People as a Servant of God.*

saturated with Nikolai's experience, as he was *personally saved by Christ and in Christ*—the experience universally shared by all true Christians from apostolic times until the present. He confirmed this sentiment around the same year that he introduced the Indian poet and philosopher Rabindranath Tagore in a lecture delivered at the University of Belgrade, where he said: "This world resembles a snake's nest, a bag full of snakes, but among them can be found an Eel. I was fortunate to have found the Eel among the snakes." Although it looks like a snake, an eel is a variety of fish and is not venomous. Also, having in mind the use of *Ichthys*, the symbol used by the early Christians (ΙΧΘΥΣ, Greek for *fish*) that can be read as an acrostic in ancient Greek "Jesus Christ, Son of God, Savior," it becomes clear that Nikolai confessed Christ as his personal Savior, which is characteristic of early believers as well as all true Christians to this day.

In his *Akathist to Christ the Conqueror of Death*, prayers that have remained unknown until the present day, Nikolai confesses reverently and poetically his Christology, which is apologetic and universal as well as evangelical and soteriological. Nowhere else as in this *Akathist* is the presence of Nikolai's understanding and experience of Christ the God-man so evident. The *Akathist's* Christology is all-encompassing, but deals mainly with soteriological, liturgical, and eschatological implications. This poetic text is rife with Orthodox theology, even Trinitarian theology, expressed in a form closer to common experience and understanding [than academic exposition]. All the elements of the Old and New Testament are present here as well as the Christological experience of early Christianity, after which follow the perception and experience of Christ from the Patristic period. Christ, here, is first and foremost the God-man and Savior. In its spirited, evangelical content, Nikolai's Christology in the *Akathist* closely resembles the exposition of faith found in Pope Leo's famed *Tomos to Flavian* (449)—even today this classic text remains a bone of contention to some Eastern Monophysites for its gospel realism, emphasizing Christ's humanity which is at the same time inseparable from His Divinity. This theological text represents the pinnacle of Western, Latin Christianity (no other Bishop of Rome has since achieved the level of theology of Pope Leo), and clearly establishes Christ as Redeemer. This is the main thrust of Nikolai's Christology not only in the *Akathist*, but in all his later works.

Such is the Christology in his classical exegetical work *The Homilies* (1925), written under the heavy influence of the Church Fathers (and often quoted there), as well as in the popular, but deeply theological and ecclesiastical work, *The Prologue of Ohrid* (1928).[6] We'll refer only to this classical passage borrowed from St. Cyril of Jerusalem:

> This is He Who Is and He Who Was, consubstantial with the Father, the Only Begotten, enthroned with the Father, equal in power, Almighty, without beginning, uncreated, immutable, indescribable, invisible, ineffable, incomprehensible, immeasurable, unfathomable, uncircumscribed. He is the *radiance of His Father's Glory* (Heb. 1:3). He is the Creator of the substance of all things created. He is the Light of Light, shining from the bosom of the Father. He is God of gods, *that such is God, Our God forever and ever* (Ps. 47:13 LXX; 48:14 KJV), and God of God who gives us knowledge of Himself. He is the Fountain of Life, *For with You is the Fountain of our life* (Ps 35:10; 36:9), flowing from the Father's Fountain of life. He is the River of God; *There is a river whose streams shall make glad the city of God* (Ps. 45:5; 46:4), *The river of God is full of water* (Ps. 64:10; 65:9), Who comes forth from the infinity of God but is not separated from Him. He is the Treasury of the Father's good gifts and endless blessings. He is the Living Water that gives life to the world. *But whoever drinks the water I shall give you will never thirst; the water I shall give you will become in him a spring of water welling up to eternal life* (John 4:14). He is the uncreated light that is begotten but not separated from the First Sun. He is God the Word (Logos); *In the beginning was the Word, and the Word was with God, and the Word was God* (John 1:1), Who with one word brought forth all things from non-existence into being. *All things came to be through Him, and without Him nothing came to be* (cf. John 1:1–3; Heb. 1:2–3; Col. 1:16). This is He Who created us in the image of God and has now made Himself man in our image (cf. Gen. 1:27; 2:5; Col. 3:10), but at the same time God!
>
> (*The Prologue of Ohrid, March 18*)

[6] *The Prologue of Ohrid* was compiled from material and experience gathered on the Holy Mountain and, like his *Homilies*, was written in the solitude of the Hilandar Monastery. From the material gathered there, Nikolai wrote these two works that differ from all his previous works, firstly, because of their ecclesiastical-evangelical spirit, and, secondly, because of their witness of Orthodox, patristic writings and experience. To speak about *The Homilies* and *The Prologue* would mean to speak about the Church Fathers, whose sayings are used by and large in these works.

A similar Christological exposition can be found in one of his many *Missionary Letters*[7] (*Letter 96*) where he gleans theological-Christological meaning from a passage in the Book of Exodus (3:14), *I Am That* ***I Am***:

> By this word "*I Am*" the Divine nature of our Lord Jesus Christ has been revealed. The Eternal Son of the Eternal Father. The Father, the Light, and the Son, the Light. God the Father and God the Son... Since God the Father is the Divine Essence, the Immutable, so is the Son of the Eternal Father. This is why the Son of God could claim about Himself: *I and My Father are One* (John 10:30)... It has been revealed that the eternal Son of God was made manifest to the world by being born of the Most Holy Virgin Mary. He put flesh on His spiritual Divine being and came into the world as man. By so doing He neither separated Himself from His eternal Parent nor ceased to be the Being, the Immutable, the Eternal, *I Am*. By assuming human nature He undergoes change: He grows up, He hungers, He suffers, He dies—but, as God, He undergoes no change. He is True God and True Man!... Even in a small human body, our great Lord was and remains the Being, the Immutable, the Eternal.

Nikolai's Sermon on Nativity from the same period (1935—there are many similar ones about Nativity and Pascha in his *Sermons and Homilies*) is where our Christologian speaks about the "uniqueness and exceptionality of God's Incarnation":

> There is but One God. There is but One Messiah (Christ). There is but One God and Messiah Who assumed flesh, and that is Jesus Christ... The exceptionality and uniqueness of the Incarnation of our Lord Jesus Christ has always been and remains the basic dogma throughout the ages.
>
> (*CW*, vol. 9, p. 90)

He reiterates this in his work *The Faith of Educated People* (1931), a work which represents his interpretation of the Church's Creed:

> The Only Begotten Son of God, the Dearest (Loved) One, bowed the heavens and descended to earth for our sake and our salva-

[7] The *Missionary Letters* were written between 1930 and 1934.

> tion... There is but One Messiah (proclaimed by God through the Prophets), our Lord Jesus Christ, the Only Begotten Son of God, the King and the Guest, born on earth from the most pure Virgin Mary. He suffered, was crucified for our sake under Pontius Pilate, and was buried. He resurrected and ascended into heaven where He is seated at the right hand of God the Father.

Immediately following this confession of faith, in the manner of a Church theologian and Christologian, Nikolai draws a characteristically Orthodox connection between Christology and Ecclesiology:

> When you believe in Christ the Savior, Christ-bearers, you believe in His work. The Work of Christ is His Church... We call the Church the Body of Christ. And Christ is the Head of the Church... Therefore: there is one Christ, one Head, one Body—one Church. (cf. 1 Cor. 12:12–13; Eph. 4:4–6)

Because of time constraints we'll limit ourselves to making the brief remark that Nikolai's Christology is tightly connected with Triadology[8] as well as Pneumatology. In his work *The Serbian People as a Servant of God* (1942), he makes the following link between Christology and Pneumatology: "Even as the Son of God Almighty, as God of God, Christ became incarnate of the Holy Spirit and Virgin Mary." Then he adds:

> The Lord Jesus, Son of God, sent the Holy Spirit to descend upon His disciples, the Spirit of Truth, the Comforter, Whom the world cannot receive. This is God the Holy Spirit, Who proceeds from the Father, and through the Son descends on people. He is of One Essence with the Father and the Son, He makes all things pure and holy, He illumines and enlightens all, unites all, strengthens all, exalts all, revives and regenerates and prepares all the faithful to become sons of the Kingdom of Heaven.

Nikolai also connects his Triadological and Christological confession of faith with the Divine *Liturgy* of the Church:

[8] E.g., *Homily on the Sunday of the Holy Fathers of the First Ecumenical Council, Sermon on The Holy Trinity* (Skoplje, 1931), *The Faith of Educated People, The Serbian People as a Servant of God, Cassiana*, etc.

> The Divine Liturgy represents the heart of the drama of the Son of God, Who was sent by the Father and was filled with the Holy Spirit. The Son of God, however, revealed Himself to people as the perfect Image of the eternal Kingdom of Heaven, that is, of the *blessed Kingdom* of the Father and the Son and the Holy Spirit. The Son of God, our Lord Jesus Christ, has revealed to us that Blessed Kingdom and invited people to prepare themselves to enter into it. This is the greatest of all discoveries in the history of the world and the most jubilant invitation extended to the human race since the beginning of time... He Himself Is the Incarnate Kingdom of Heaven.
>
> (*CW*, vol. 13, pp. 38–39)

Elsewhere in his writings, speaking about the Divine Liturgy, Nikolai says:

> The word Liturgy means *Public duty*. That is, the work of Christ's love that is given to all people who accept that love and respond with love. It does not mean a public concept, or a public idea, but a *Public duty*... Christ sacrificed Himself wholly for the sake of all, and remained whole. Christ gave everything that was His as well as Himself, and gained everything. Therefore He said, *All authority in heaven and on earth has been given to Me* (Matt. 28:18). Christ was victorious in all battles, He collected all spoils of war and released captives from prison (cf. Eph. 4:8–10; 1 Pet. 3:18–22).
>
> (*The Serbian People as a Servant of God*, pp. 29–30)

These are all liturgical, eucharistical expressions that Nikolai draws upon from the Liturgy of St. Basil the Great. This is why in *The Serbian People as a Servant of God* he continues, "By importance, the New Testament is the rule of *service* (i.e., *liturgy*) to God, and is holy, perfect and uncompromising. *For the Son of God did not come to be served, but to serve* (Matt. 20:28)." He finishes this work with the words: "The Liturgy is the confirmation of love for people. With His Liturgy, God confirmed His love for mankind... For this reason everything—in Orthodoxy and with Orthodox Serbs—is closely linked with Christ's Liturgy."

Not incidentally, it is a well-known fact that Bishop Nikolai was entirely a man of prayer, of service and [a fervent celebrant of] the Divine

Liturgy. He wrote numerous prayers and church services, including the renowned three prayers written immediately after his release from the Dachau prison camp. In one of them, he addresses Christ the Savior in his characteristic way: "Christ our Lord, our Teacher, our Redeemer, our Resurrection, our Triumph over Satan and death, the Lover of men, You are God of all our Fathers and all Holy Martyrs." These last words take us to another directly connected theme of Nikolai's Theology and Christology, and that is the vibrant Orthodox Church *Tradition*.

> The Apostles and Holy Fathers of the Church understood well Christ's teaching on prayer... The Holy Fathers, as the immediate descendants of the Holy Apostles, compiled prayers (i.e., *Liturgical prayers*) in accordance with time-tested experience... The Orthodox Church maintains that experience under the name of Holy Tradition. And Holy Tradition is the most progressive thing in the world, for it confirms the Holy Scriptures century after century, and generation after generation... We do not add to the Holy Scriptures. We add to the Holy Tradition with every new experience and spiritual treasure (i.e., *from the Holy Spirit*) that sheds more light on God's Holy Scriptures. It is because of her immensely abundant *Tradition* that the Orthodox Church is the most progressive of all Churches. Without Holy Tradition it is difficult to understand the Bible as the Book of Life.
>
> (*The Serbian People as a Servant of God*)

This vibrant Holy Tradition of the Orthodox Church is seen first and foremost in her ascetic and liturgical experience. It is through God's grace that it has been revealed and given to us to experience her vibrant liturgical life, prayer, the Eucharistic Mystery, and asceticism. It is through Christ's New Testament and in His Church—His Body—and by participation in *His Public Work* that we discover this Tradition. That is why Nikolai, time and again, wrote in his *Notebooks* the famous words: "Life, life, life—the most frequently repeated word (and reality) in the New Testament—is the high tenor of the New Testament, the main string in the Christian Harp."

The great witness and life-long bearer of the life of Christ in the Church was and remains our Nikolai, the Holy Bishop of Ohrid and Zhicha. His words about St. Seraphim of Sarov apply equally to him: "The teaching is not new, but the *Saint is*; the religion is not new, but the experience is. In a word, here is a new Witness and a confirmation of faith."

Many more things could be said about Nikolai's Christology, especially from two of his short but, in our opinion, the best and most theologically inspired of his works: *Cassiana* and *The Century (or Hundred Chapters) from Ljubostinja*. In *Cassiana* we find the essence of the Christian understanding of God—the Holy Trinity—as Love (not in the *psychological* but in the *ontological* meaning of the word), and of Christ as the Loved Son of God and Son of Man; the Savior and God-man; in the Church and with the Church, or even *as the Church*. It is about the theanthropic *Mystery/Event* that is Christ (i.e., the Church) which Nikolai so eloquently writes in *The Century from Ljubostinja*, part of a larger work entitled *The Century on Orthodoxy*.

Although Nikolai's last work, *The Only Lover of Mankind*, indicates that Christ remains his primary literary theme, the aforementioned two works, *Cassiana* and *The Century*, are nevertheless the best, the most concise, and the most profound exposition of the *Christological mystery* of that very same *Lover of Mankind*—Jesus Christ—Who is the *Same* yesterday, today, and forever (Heb. 13:8).

Athanasius (Yevtich),
retired Bishop of Hercegovina
Translated by Teodora Simic

St. Nikolai of Zhicha: A Contemporary Orthodox Witness

by Bishop Irinej (Dobrijevic)

Preface

Given the unique proportions of a life lived in Christ by this divinely inspired and charismatic, erudite individual, it difficult to encompass the vast expanse of his unique witness to Orthodoxy within the given limitations of a single presentation. Therefore, myself hailing from America, I have chosen an aspect of his life, which is singularly particular to him: His religious and socio-political witness to America, and the response of his American contemporaries, institutions and media to him the person, and to his message. The focal point of this presentation will be Nikolai's three distinct American missions: 1915, 1921, and 1927, which are as relevant today as they were in their time.

Introduction

His academic background is scholarly and distinguished. He was a prolific writer and an eloquent orator; an inspired theologian and poet; a prophet and a visionary; a mystic and an apologist; an effective archpastor and intellectual; and a skilled diplomat and a Christian statesman. He was, without a doubt, the harmonious embodiment of faith and culture, Christianity and patriotism. The testimony of this unique individual has been the subject of many writings. In the Serbian Orthodox Church, he is regarded as the "New Chrysostom." To his American contemporaries, he was known as a "Second Isaiah."

Bishop Nikolai's collective works have been assembled into an encyclopedic set of volumes, spanning the various languages and traditions he had come to master. Nikolai was fluent in seven languages. His works always evoke the eternal and never the temporary. Each work is universal, including within itself various and diverse elements and covering numerous aspects and concerns. Nikolai was himself the patristic embodiment of an Orthodox intellectual, philanthropist, and hierarch, freely lecturing in the halls of the world's most pre-eminent universities, and as comfortable addressing royalty as the simplest of his faithful flock. As Nikolai himself so often chose to note, his was a "diocese without geographic boundaries."

1915—America

With the outbreak of World War I, in the summer of 1914, the Balkan Peninsula was hurled into complete and utter turmoil. The Serbian nation was in dire need of a charismatic leader to help them calm this international crisis. For this purpose, the young Archimandrite Nikolai was commissioned on an official diplomatic mission to England and the United States to recruit support for the suffering Serbian people. He was received with full honor and dignity. Nikolai effectively displayed his keen political astuteness not only in addressing the issue of the Serbs, but also by directing his attention to the cause of world peace and methodologies given to political ideals. At his influence, the British Parliament voted to accept the emerging South Slav State into the League of Nations.

By late summer of 1915, Archimandrite Nikolai arrived in America together with Dr. Dushan Grgin; Raka Majstorovich, a chemical plant director; Lt. Col. Jevrem Popovich; and eighteen other young men, who were to review and receive military materials.[1] Their express purpose was to gather the émigré Serbs, Croats, and Slovenes in solidarity, given their common plight in the Austro-Hungarian Empire, from which many had fled to America. The then Metropolitan Dimitrije of Belgrade also charged Nikolai with visiting all of the Serbian parishes in America, having secured permission for the same from Archbishop Evdokim of the Aleutian Islands and North America, being that the Serbian parishes were under the jurisdiction of the Russian Orthodox Mission of North America.

On August 29, 1915, Archimandrite Nikolai together with Professor Michael Idvorsky Pupin of Columbia University, honorary Serbian Consul General to the United States, chaired a historic meeting at the Amsterdam Opera House in New York City, the thrust of which was to evoke sympathy for the Serbian nation in view of its plight during the

[1] Bishop Sava of Shumadija, "Misija jeromonaha dr. Nikolaia Velimirovicha u Americi 1915" [The mission of hieromonk Dr. Nikolai Velimirovich in America 1915], in *Kalendar crkva* [Church calendar] (Belgrade, 1990), pp. 89–90.

current war. From this gathering, a resolution was drafted and forwarded to President Woodrow Wilson confirming their support for the Allies.[2]

Archimandrite Nikolai's mission was overwhelmingly successful. America sent over twenty thousand freedom-loving Slavic volunteers, most of who fought heroically on the Salonica Front, and later became known as "The Third Army of Bishop Nikolai." Additionally, hundreds of thousands of dollars in aid was sent to their suffering brethren in their Fatherland.

In a dream, during the course of this trip, he received a message from an Angel of the Lord, revealing to him that he would someday return to America in order to organize the growing Serbian Orthodox communities. Following his visit, Nikolai became convinced that the Serbs in America rightfully deserved to be united with their Mother Church in Belgrade. It was his firm conviction that a Serbian bishop should be elected to form a new diocese in America and Canada. Due to the war, at that time, this plan was not realized, as the Holy Assembly of Bishops of the Serbian Orthodox Church was unable to convene in session.

Nikolai took advantage of this initial American visit to travel extensively throughout the country. At every major city which he visited, Nikolai delivered outstanding homilies and speeches that captivated his American audiences. The Serbs of Chicago were recorded as having been emotionally roused to the point of giving him a standing ovation, noting: "For those were flaming words interwoven with the Gospel, the Way of St. Sava and Serbian nationalism."

According to Canon Edward N. West,[3] prior to the 1915 arrival of Archimandrite Nikolai, the Anglican Communion viewed with remoteness the "exotic Eastern Orthodox Faith." In his "Recollections of Bishop Nikolai," he writes how it was Nikolai who was uniquely responsible for the unveiling of Orthodoxy to the various Christian denominations, both in Britain, where he electrified the Church of England, and in the United States:

"The First World War brought a sudden and profound concern for the imperially throttled Serbs... The Archimandrite Nikolai Velimirovich came, and in three months left an impression that continues to this day. His vision of the Church as God's family, as over against God's empire,

[2] "Many Slavs Here Declare for Allies," *New York Times*, August 30, 1915.

[3] I believe Canon West to have commissioned the first known icon of Bishop Nikolai, which became the standard for most of the later icons.

simply shattered the West's notion of what it had regarded as the Caesaro-Papism of Eastern Orthodoxy."[4]

1921—America

Given the background of his 1915 visit to the United States, and his gained reputation as a powerful and eloquent orator, the now Right Reverend Bishop Nikolai of Zhicha was invited by various universities in the United States, such as Columbia University in New York City and the Protestant Episcopal Church, to visit America. He was to present a lecture tour to the universities and deliver homilies in the various churches. At the personal invitation of his life-long friend the Rev. Dr. William Manning, whom he befriended in 1915, Nikolai was also invited to attend his consecration as the tenth Episcopal Bishop of New York.

Known for his love of children, his indefatigable and fatherly concern for the poor of his diocese, Nikolai was in like manner extended an invitation by the Council of Serbian Child Welfare to travel to America. It was anticipated, given the success of his first visit, that he would be of major assistance to them in collecting funds for Serbia and possibly in establishing orphanages for the unfortunate war orphans, both in the United States and in Serbia. Over six hundred children would eventually be the recipients of his manifested love of Christ, as Nikolai managed, again, to secure thousands of dollars for the care of the "little ones." To the poor children of Serbia, he became an endearing figure, affectionately called *"Deda Vladika"* (Grandfather Bishop).

With the backing of the Royal Yugoslav Government and the Holy Synod of Bishops, Nikolai was commissioned to travel to the United States, and given the additional missionary task of gathering the scattered Serbian communities into an organized Serbian Orthodox Church in America. A letter of introduction was sent to Archbishop Alexander of the Aleutian Islands and North America by the now Patriarch Dimitrije of Serbia to explain the nature of Bishop Nikolai's visit, requesting that they receive him, and that he not be hindered in the execution of his work.

On January 24, 1921, Bishop Nikolai arrived in the United States of America, where he was to remain for the following six months. During the course of his stay, he delivered approximately 140 lectures and homi-

[4] *1979 Calendar of the Serbian Orthodox Church in the USA and Canada* (Chicago: The Clergy Brotherhood), p. 84.

lies in America's finest universities and cathedrals, as well as in smaller parish churches and missionary congregations. Wherever he traveled, Nikolai was fondly and warmly received, never intimidating anyone with the wellspring of his vast knowledge. For, as Professor Dr. Veselin Kesich wrote of him:

> Bishop Nikolai knew that men are afraid of the heights and the depths of thought and therefore wanted to simplify everything and equalize all things. [However] he fights the reduction of religion to a common denominator... There is the awareness of God's presence; there is the touch of the divine in his works.[5]

On February 8, 1921, Bishop Nikolai, on behalf of the Council of Serbian Child Welfare, addressed the student assembly at Columbia University in New York City. As recorded in the *New York Times*,[6] Bishop Nikolai blamed the "methodologies" of the European universities for the past World War. His claims were based on the fact that a specific thought system was developed throughout the nineteenth century in which European universities created an artificial intellectual class, which could only relate to material possessions. It was then this very same artificial intelligentsia which led Europe into the First World War, and is today preparing Europe for yet another war. Serbia, he noted, is in such a state that it "cannot recover entirely because all Europe is sick." In a concluding message, Nikolai, speaking as a prophet in their midst, reading the signs of his times, warned Columbia University that their educational methodologies were also in the process of leading to another war.

In response to Bishop Nikolai's lecture, a fierce debate raged on the pages of the New York press. In a letter to the editor of the *New York Times*,[7] dated February 9, 1921, L. Duguit, Dean of the Faculty of Law at Bordeaux University in France, who at the time was a visiting professor at Columbia University, strongly protested the Bishop's remarks. Duguit felt it his obligation to make this protest in the name of French universities and particularly the faculties of law in France, asserting that they have always promoted "right over might" and that the greatness of a nation lies in the moral

[5] "In Memoriam: Bishop Nikolai Velimirovich," *The Russian Orthodox Journal*, vol. 31, no. 1 (New York, May 1957), p. 5.

[6] "Blames Europe's Colleges," *New York Times*, February 9, 1921.

[7] "Universities and the War," *New York Times*, February 14, 1921.

values which it spreads in the world. On the contrary, he insisted that the French universities had done everything to prevent the past war.

In defense of the Bishop, an initialed author, "J. A.," wrote a letter to the editor of the *New York Times*[8] on February 15, 1921. He contended that such dismissing attacks on Nikolai's Columbia statement were a "dead issue," while the issue raised by the Bishop was indeed a "very live issue," in that, "no one has yet finished the war." He found Nikolai's thesis to be both interesting and logical. Concluding his letter to the editor, the writer noted that despite the terrible state in which his Serbian people are, Nikolai did not once seek American aid for Serbia. Rather, his plea was for the assistance of all humanity—America included.

An interesting historical aside to this debate is that the same Columbia University in 1946, after the Second World War, was to grant Bishop Nikolai a Doctorate of Sacred Theology *honoris causa*, with the following citation:

> The Right Reverend Nikolai Velimirovich, Bishop of Ohrida and Zhicha of the Serbian Orthodox Church, known and revered for his saintliness and charity; thinking first always of the poor and the unfortunate in a country which has suffered much; a great scholar, a great preacher, and, above all, a great moral force. Degree awarded *Honoris Causa*.[9]

Prior to the conclusion of his lecture tour, Nikolai, who had roused the curious eye of the American media, was requested to publish his personal, socio-political interpretations of America: past, present and future. Titled, "A Serbian's View of America," these perspective writings were published in the *New York Evening Post* and *The Living Church* on June 4 and 25, 1921, respectively. The thrust of these articles was to compare post–World War I Europe, with its intrigues, to a dawning, young, and potentially superior America.

Europe has discovered the world. Can America organize it, asks the Bishop? According to him, organization continues to be the "watchword of our time." However, he warns: "The organization of anything must begin at the beginning—with the organization of my own soul and yours."[10]

[8] "Bishop Nikolai's Appeal," *New York Times,* February 18, 1921.

[9] Columbian Collection: Columbia University, New York, 1946.

[10] *Ibid.*

Practicing what he preached, and truly a witness to Orthodoxy, Nikolai accepted to pay an unusual pastoral visit to an African-American Congregation, St. Philip's Church in Harlem. On Paschal Monday 1921, he was greeted by 1,400 parishioners and forty outside students. The community proudly displayed both American and Serbian flags. Following his delivery on love towards one's neighbor, which unites all nations and manifests itself in the equality of all races, the entire congregation rose and sang the Serbian national anthem. The far-reaching consequences of this visit were evident twenty-five years later. Grayed and fatigued by Dachau, the well-remembered Nikolai would enjoy freely strolling down the then dangerous streets of Harlem as the eager young African-American children would run to kiss his hands and receive candy from him.

Nikolai was also invited to address the clergy of America on many and varied occasions. A luncheon was held in his honor by the Clergy Club of New York on April 12, 1921, at the Pennsylvania Hotel. One of the featured speakers was Archbishop Meletios of Athens and All Greece. Bishop Nikolai openly criticized Americans for their levity, claiming,

> You are too much given to laughing men in America because you do not realize the agony of the world. We are weeping too much there [in Europe]. America has not yet spoken.
>
> When those statesmen sat about that table and tried to make peace, they all relied on their human power. And it was not peace. There is no peace now, and the world is thirsting, hungering for peace.
>
> It is impossible to have a League of Nations. Lawyers have tried to establish a league of nations on the Roman law. You can't form Christian nations on the basis of Caesar.[11]

Whether addressing august gatherings of this sort, or authoring articles to the American clergy, Nikolai's message was always consistently the same:

> Can the Churches in America, speaking with one voice, as strong as many waters, inspire with conviction the leaders of the Christian nations? To be able to do this all Church leaders must awaken to apocalyptic earnestness of the present time, and must feel like sol-

[11] "Raps American Levity," *New York Times,* April 13, 1921.

> diers in different uniforms, but all of the same army, marching toward the same goal... All power is in Christ. The world today stands powerless. Why does it not organize itself? What is it waiting for? Well, the organization of the world depends on the revival and organization of the Church. The Church organization depends on the hearts of Church leaders. There is the key. A superhuman effort is necessary for all Church leaders to overcome themselves for Christ's sake and thereby for humanity's sake. Is not America already used to superhuman effort?[12]

Finally, concerning the formation of a Serbian Orthodox Church in the United States of America and Canada, Bishop Nikolai, as the first Serbian hierarch to visit America, wrote a 1921 *Paschal Encyclical* to all of the Serbian parishes in the United States. In this historically important document, he conveys the greetings of Patriarch Dimitrije to the faithful Serbian flock in the Dispersion. Having already visited most of the Serbian parishes and investigated their pastoral needs, he stressed the importance of uniting the scattered Serbian flock under the jurisdiction of the Serbian Patriarchate.

On September 21, 1921, Bishop Nikolai was appointed as the first Serbian Bishop to administer in America. He remained in this capacity until 1923, when Archimandrite Mardarije Uskokovich was consecrated as the first resident bishop in America.

1927—America

At the invitation of the American Yugoslav Society, the Institute of Politics in Williamstown, Massachusetts, and the Carnegie Endowment for International Peace, Bishop Nikolai once again was invited to travel to America in 1927. The purpose of this trip was to deliver a series of lectures on world peace at the Institute of Politics at Williams College. In addition, during his two months here, he was scheduled to deliver sermons in both Episcopalian and Orthodox churches; lecture at Princeton University; and speak before the Federal Council of Churches in New York City.

Dr. James T. Shotwell of the Carnegie Endowment for International Peace announced the anticipated arrival of Bishop Nikolai to America

12 "A Message from Bishop Nikolai to American Church Leaders," *The Living Church* (Milwaukee: May 14, 1921), p. 1.

on Sunday, August 5, 1927, by describing him as "one of the most interesting and picturesque public figures in the political life of the Balkan States... By temperament a mystic, but by proved capacity a trained diplomat and statesman, Bishop Nikolai presents a combination that would make him an outstanding figure in any country."[13]

Speaking before a group of New York City businessmen and professionals, representatives of the Institute of Politics, and reporters for the *New York Times*, Bishop Nikolai stated that this was his third visit to America: "The first time he studied its prosperity, the second visit was to observe its charities, and this time he has come to study its possibilities." In outlining his plan for world peace, which would actively include American participation, predicated upon the basis of Christian spirituality, he noted:

> I come to advocate a world peace based on spiritual rights rather than upon material forces. All other mediums have failed to bring about peace, and it now seems fair to give Christianity the opportunity... The United States has not shared in the League of Nations, nor has it shared in the Locarno Pact. Now the civilized world looks to America to give her opinion, for it has not yet spoken. May it not be on the basis of Christianity?[14]

His theme of spiritual revival was also heard at the Cathedral Church of St. John the Divine, on August 7, 1927, where Nikolai delivered a sermon on the problem of "East and West." He maintained that one of the greatest world problems today is the relationship between East and West. He likened the division to two twins, separated and suspicious of each other:

> The East says it represents wisdom and the West says it represents power... What is wrong with the East is that it lacks divine revelation. What is wrong with the West is that it lacks divine inspiration... What we need today most of all is that Christ's revealed wisdom should rectify and vivify the Wisdom of the East, and that His divine inspiration should spiritualize the power of the West.[15]

13 "Jugoslav Bishop Coming to America," *New York Times,* July 4, 1927.

14 "Bishop Nikolai Here to Advocate Peace," *New York Times*, August 6, 1927.

15 "Bishop Nikolai of Serbia Preaches at Cathedral of St. John the Divine," *The Living Church* (Milwaukee: August 20, 1927), pp. 539–40.

Bishop Nikolai's involvement with the Serbian Church was extremely limited during this visit. This was done to prevent dissension among the Serbs, since there were factions continually seeking him to take up permanent residence in America. Regarding this visit, Rev. Dr. H. Henry Spoer of the Episcopalian Church commented:

> The coming among us of the Bishop of Ohrida is an event of consequence to our Church as well as his own... In spite of their large numbers, and their prosperous conditions here, the people of the Serbian Church have need of our sympathy and of our practical cooperation. Bishop Nikolai comes as a guest of the Carnegie Endowment for International Peace. The message, which he brings from his Church to ours is that of brotherly love. It is for us to do our part.[16]

Conclusion

Perhaps Bishop Nikolai's three American missions are most aptly summarized in his own words, written in retrospect, towards the close of his own life, lived out in America:

> I have come from an Old to this New World. Which is the better; the Old or the New? I could not know. But the Revealer of all truths has said to me and to you, that a wise householder brings forth equally new and old things out of his treasury: Not only the new, and not only the old, but both. Our Lord Jesus respected the Old Testament, but at the same time He revealed the New one. Now we, His followers, are keeping both as one Holy Book. The highest wisdom consists in keeping both old and new treasures. The separation of the two brings poverty, instability and confusion.[17]

IRINEJ (Dobrijevic)
Bishop of Australia and New Zealand
The Serbian Orthodox Church

[16] "Ohrida, and the Serbian Church in America," *The Living Church* (Milwaukee: September 3, 1927), p. 588.

[17] "New and Old Treasures," *Orthodoxy: Herald of the Serbian Orthodox Church* (October–December 1960), pp. 41–42.

Appendix I

Prayer LXXV from *Prayers by the Lake*

by St. Nikolai Velimirovich

Bless my enemies, O Lord. And I bless them and do not curse them.

My enemies have driven me into Your arms more than my friends have. My friends have bound me to the earth; my enemies have loosened my bonds from the earth and have destroyed all my hopes in the world.

They have turned me into a stranger in these earthly realms and into a unneeded inhabitant of this earth. Just as a hunted animal finds safer shelter then when it is not pursued, so have I, hunted down by my enemies, found the safest shelter by hiding under Your tabernacle where neither friend nor foe can slay my soul. Bless my enemies, O Lord. And I bless them and do not curse them.

They, rather than I, have confessed my sins before the world.

They flogged me, when I hesitated to flog myself.

They vexed me, when I tried to flee suffering.

They scolded me, when I flattered myself.

They spat upon me, when I took pride in myself.

Bless my enemies, O Lord. And I bless them and do not curse them.

When I pretended to be wise, they called me a fool.

When I pretended to be mighty, they mocked me as a dwarf.

When I wanted to lead the people, they pushed me into the background.

When I rushed to enrich myself, they prevented me with an iron hand.

When I thought that I could sleep peacefully, they awoke me from my slumber.

When I built a home for a long and tranquil life, they demolished it and drove me out.

Truly, my enemies have loosened my bonds from the world and have stretched out my hands to the hem of Your garment.

Bless my enemies, O Lord. And I bless them and do not curse them.

Bless them and multiply them; multiply them and embitter them even more against me,

so that my flight to You may have no return,

so that my hope in men may be rent asunder like cobwebs,

so that complete serenity may reign in my soul,

so that my heart may become the grave of my two evils twins: arrogance and anger,

so that I might gather all my treasure in heaven.

Ah, so that I may for once be freed from self-deception, which has entangled me in the dreadful web of this illusory life.

My enemies have made known to me—what only a few know—that a person has no enemies in this world other than himself.

One hates his enemies only when he fails to realize that they are not enemies but cruel friends.

Truly, it is difficult for me to say who has done me greater good and greater evil in this world: my friends or foes.

Therefore, bless, O Lord, my friends and foes.

A slave curses his enemies, for he does not understand. But a son blesses them, for he has understanding.

For a son knows that his enemies cannot touch his life. Hence, he walks freely among them and prays to God for them.

Bless my enemies, O Lord. And I bless and do not curse them.

Monastery of St. Nahum, Ohrid

Appendix II

Preface to *Serbia in Light and Darkness*[1]

by Randall Davidson, the Archbishop of Canterbury

The presence of Father Nikolai Velimirovich in England during the last few months has brought to the many circles with which he has been in touch a new message and appeal enforced by a personality evoking an appreciation which glows more warmly the better he is known. But this little book is more than the revelation of a personality. It will be to many people the introduction to a new range of interest and of thought. He would be a bold man who would endeavour at present to limit or even to define what may be the place which the Serbia of coming years may hold in Eastern Europe as a link between peoples who have been widely sundered and between forces both religious and secular which for their right understanding have needed an interpreter. Of recent days the sculpture and literature of Serbia have been brought to our doors, and England's admiration for both has drawn the two countries more closely together in the common struggle for the ideals to which that art and literature have sought to give expression. It is not, I think, untrue to say that to the average English home this unveiling of Serbia has been an altogether new experience. Father Nikolai's book will help to give to the revelation a lasting place in their minds, their hopes and their prayers.

Randall Cantuar[2]
Lambeth, Easter 1916

[1] Nikolai Velimirovich, *Serbia in Light and Darkness* (London: Longmans, Green and Co., 1916; repr., New York: Cosimo Classics, 2007).—Ed.

[2] Cantuar: from the Latin for "Canterbury."—Ed.